THE
MOLLY MAGUIRES

BY ANTHONY BIMBA

INTERNATIONAL PUBLISHERS

NEW YORK

PUBLISHER'S NOTE

This is the first book to have revealed the true nature of the so-called Molly Maguires of the Pennsylvania anthracite region as pioneers and martyrs in the early efforts to organize the coal miners. Although originally published in 1932, the new studies appearing since then and using new source materials not available to the author confirm Anthony Bimba's basic findings.

It may be justly surmised that this early work inspired the subsequent books on the "Mollies"—and even a full-length motion picture released in 1970. But none of the newer books set forth so clearly and unequivocally as in this study the role of the railroad company which owned the mines in organizing the terror in the coalfields and managing the frame-up trial which sent the "Mollies" to the gallows. Employing the smoothest and most dramatic effects, Hollywood has managed to obscure completely the criminal complicity of the railroad company, whose president hired the Pinkerton spies and provocateurs and acted as state prosecutor in the trials. Perhaps with the new interest aroused by the movie, many will want to discover the real facts.

PREFACE

THE American working class has a background of militant struggle. Each labor struggle, occurring under special conditions and having its own peculiar features, has contributed to a rich tradition of militancy. As a whole the American workers remain unaware of this background, although they are building up and adding to this tradition in the tremendous struggles of to-day. These new struggles, having their setting in the unprecedented economic crisis, have a tendency to be set apart from all that has gone before. It therefore becomes very urgent to reconstruct the labor struggles of the past from the point of view of the most recent developments so that those workers who are in the forefront of the struggles to-day may see them as a continuous development of the struggles of yesterday, become acquainted with their own traditions and gain the full perspective of the developing movement of the American working class.

This task is made difficult because many of the earlier struggles have been almost entirely neglected or forgotten by the labor movement, leaving the field clear for unsympathetic or openly hostile writers and historians. Thus, many of these events have been buried under mountains of misrepresentations and calumnies or handed down in a completely distorted form. Much of the material relating to these events must be excavated and the "forgotten chapters" in the history of the American working class be reconstructed. With the misrepresentations exposed and discarded these struggles will take their rightful place in the traditions of the working class and help mature its class consciousness and sense of historical direction.

5

The early struggle led by the so-called Molly Maguires is one of those most neglected by the labor movement and most vilified by hostile writers. The author has attempted to reconstruct and restore this struggle to the important place which is its due in the militant traditions of labor.

The author has traveled through the anthracite region of Pennsylvania and has availed himself of the records of the Molly Maguire trials and other documents in the libraries and historical societies of the anthracite counties. Most of the other material relating directly to the Mollies was only available in the distorted accounts of those who took an active part in the struggle on the side of the coal operators and railroad companies and could only be utilized after a careful separation of the substance from the dross. The author makes no pretense of having presented a complete picture of either that period in American history in which the struggle was molded, or of the Molly Maguires themselves.

Of special value, both for the wealth of material uncovered and in tracing the main outlines of the struggle of the anthracite miners in the early period for better conditions, was Alexander Trachtenberg's *History of Legislation for the Protection of Coal Miners in Pennsylvania*. With the author's permission and aid, I drew liberally upon this study in treating of the conditions in the anthracite.

I wish to thank, among others, Melvin P. Levy and Sol Auerbach for their aid in the final editing of the manuscript. Some of their suggestions were incorporated in the contents and others were of great help in formulating my own ideas and in shaping the material. The responsibility for all that is contained in this book, however, rests entirely upon me.

ANTHONY BIMBA.

May, 1932.

CONTENTS

ILLUSTRATIONS

THOMAS DUFFY

EDWARD J. KELLY

THOMAS MUNLEY

JAMES CARROLL

MICHAEL J. DOYLE

Executed leaders of the Pennsylvania anthracite miners.

CHAPTER I

THE REAL MOLLY MAGUIRES

POPULAR legends are still extant about the "Molly Maguires." Although at least nineteen men died on the gallows as Mollies, there was no organization by that name. Both the organization and the name were invented by the mine owners and those who served them in order to provide a convenient label for the militant miners in the Pennsylvania anthracite fields. After the label itself had been made sufficiently fatal to send a man to the gallows, the mine owners proceeded to fasten this label upon all miners' leaders they wished to get rid of. It was a fiction created in the course of a fierce class battle. Like many other similar fabrications it has been embalmed in bourgeois texts and in volumes of the sensational "fictional-fact" kind as having actual historical existence of a character assigned to it by those who created the label.

Even the *History of Schuylkill County*, published in 1881, purporting to be a complete history of the county in which the struggle centered, is forced to admit that "in this county no association was organized under the name of Molly Maguires." [1] Although at least one historian assures us that it "terrorized whole counties in Pennsylvania and left a blood-red trail behind it in the coal regions of the Keystone State," nowhere in our investigation have we found it possible to lay hands on a single authentic document which showed the existence of a group or an organization calling itself the Molly Maguires.

"A deal of wild talk was said, and a deal of random writing found its way into print, about the 'terrible organization of the Molly Maguires,'" says the *Irish World,* a nationalist Irish publication appearing in New York during the upheaval of the seventies and sympathetic to the miners. The article asks pertinent questions and traces the origin of the fiction down to its source:

How many of the editors of the country set to work to examine into the truth or the falsity of that report of the agents of the coal ring lords? How many of them asked themselves the question: "Does there in reality exist such a body of men, as an organization, or is it all a myth?" How many editors put this question to themselves? Not six! They took all for granted. Their readers, in turn, took it for granted. But was there any reason for questioning the existence of such a society? Was there reason to suppose that the coal ring's emissaries had originated the phrase? Could the coal ring itself have an object in view in fabricating anything of the kind? Yes! This coal ring—which has striven and which still endeavors to reduce the miners to a condition actually worse than serfdom—found it necessary for its purpose to frighten the country with a bugbear. There are people who believe in fairies and hobgoblins. There are people who will accept any story, no matter how absurd, without ever once taking the trouble to investigate into its composition or tracing back its origin. So it was in this case. This bugbear was labeled "Molly Maguire." Sneak detectives were then engaged to discover a "mare's nest"—to discover deeds of violence which they themselves had in some instances actually planned—deeds in the complicity in which they themselves brazenly boasted on the witness stand! [2]

Who were these men whom the coal ring labeled Molly Maguires and whom bourgeois and "labor" historians alike have branded murderers and assassins?

They were miners, chiefly Irish, in the anthracite coal regions of Pennsylvania, organized into a union, the Work-

ingmen's Benevolent Association. They were also members
of an Irish fraternal association, the Ancient Order of
Hibernians. Those designated as Molly Maguires by the
coal interests were Hibernians in the miners' union who put
up a determined struggle against conditions of starvation
and peonage in the coal fields. The Irish miners of the
A. O. H. were the backbone of the union. And thereby
hinges their crime. Sweeping aside the mist of mine owners'
calumnies and lies there stands revealed the militant working-class fighter, Molly Maguire, if you wish, but minus
the sensational cutthroat prototype of the devil popularized
by the workers' enemies.

Irishmen of all classes belonged to the Ancient Order of
Hibernians. The national organization, with headquarters
in New York, was controlled by the Irish bourgeoisie and the
Catholic clergy and, therefore, had nothing in common with
the real interests of the Irish workers. While these na-
tionalists declared themselves opposed to British rule in
Ireland, they did not as much as pretend opposition to the
exploiters of Irish and other workers in the United States.
On the contrary, the national leadership of the A. O. H.
joined hands with the hangmen against the anthracite
miners. The *History of the Schuylkill County, Pa.*, by
Schalck and Henning, points out that the national convention of the A. O. H., held in April, 1877, "denounced them
[the Molly Maguires] in the strongest terms, denied their
membership in the fraternity, and . . . cut off from membership the entire territory in which they were operating."
(Vol. I, p. 164.)

In the anthracite regions of Pennsylvania the situation
was different. In spite of their mixed composition, the
branches or locals of the Ancient Order of Hibernians were
dominated by the miners themselves, who transformed the
mutual aid organization into their principal organ of class

struggle while the union itself was being smashed. The middle-class politicians of the organization were shoved into the background; the Catholic clergy openly aligned itself with the coal operators. The only organized power left opposing the coal interests was the local A. O. H. organization of the miners. The destruction of this organization, therefore, became imperative to the operators.

The employers used every means at their command to accomplish this purpose. A campaign of vituperation was started; the label "Molly Maguire," with all its ruling class distortions, was created; spies, provocateurs and gangsters were put to work. The gallows, with the dangling bodies of its victims, capped the successful campaign.

The appellation "Molly Maguire" seems to have been imported from Ireland where it found its origin in the struggle of the Irish peasants against the English landlords. One of the revolutionary peasant societies, the story goes, was called Molly Maguires; some say because it was organized by a woman of that name, others, because its members wore women's clothes during the attacks upon the landlords and the agents of the government. The Molly Maguires, as almost all societies of the Irish poor at the time, pursued a merciless struggle against the landlords and the English oppressors. They were accordingly dubbed murderers and assassins and this convenient handle was imported by the coal interests together with the name itself.

The operators had the support of the entire ruling class of America in their attack on the coal miners. The press felt the significance of the combat in the mining region and utilized the opportunity for a nation-wide attack upon workers in struggle. Not only miners, but workers throughout the country, wherever they struck or fought the employers with courage and determination, were labeled Molly Maguires, criminals and murderers. Class feeling was at a high pitch in the United States of the late seventies. The country was in the throes of a sharp economic crisis which began in 1873 and the capitalist class, as usual, attempted to shift the burden of the crisis to the working class in the form of unemployment, wage cuts and longer working hours. Workers in many industries heroically fought against these attempts to lower their standard of living, and their resistance was furiously denounced in the entire capitalist press.

Newspapers in all parts of the country picked up the Molly Maguire cry and turned it to advantage in local class battles. Strikers in New Jersey were treated to screaming headlines by the *New York Herald* in its issues of May 7 and 8, 1876: "Dynamite Explosion; A Horrid Plot; The Explosion on Bergen's Heights Caused by Strikers; New Jersey Laborers Following the Methods of the Molly Maguires." Editorially, the same newspaper demanded the blood of the Jersey City Molly Maguires!

The miners of Ohio, striking against wage reductions of from 75 to 65 cents per ton, were likewise branded Mollies by the *Herald*. The miners had mass picketed the mine, beat up the mine owner and demanded that strike-breakers quit work. That was sufficient to make out of them "Molly Maguires" of the most desperate type. When the bituminous miners on the Pan Handle Railroad struck for an advance of half a cent a bushel, the *Pittsburgh Gazette,* February 8, 1876, wrote: "Those who refused to pay the advance have been compelled to keep a force of watchmen at night to keep their property from being burned down. The four men who were employed at Brier Hill tipple on Friday night were surrounded by a force of the Molly Maguires, and an indiscriminate fire kept up on them for more than an hour."

The task of clinching the argument, however, is left to

the *New York Times,* which on May 14, 1876, carried an editorial similar to present-day anti-"Red" harangues:

The Molly Maguires have long been suspected of many violent crimes. It now seems that from burning "coal-breakers" and mobbing men who were willing to work for wages under the rate demanded by strikers, the rise to darker deeds was easy and natural. The trade unions of England have resorted to murder, assassination and arson, in order to strike terror into the hearts of those who oppose them. This root of evil has been planted on American soil, and in the mining regions of Pennsylvania we see the legitimate fruit. . . . The Pennsylvania authorities owe it to civilization to exterminate this noxious growth, now that its roots have been discovered.

The impression which the employers desired to create with the help of Molly Maguirism is succinctly summarized in one sentence by the *American Law Review* of January, 1877: "The chief business of the employed (workers) is to engage in strikes and to commit crime."

Thus we see that the "Molly Maguires" were to be found not only in the anthracite coal regions of Pennsylvania, but wherever struggles took place between workers and employers. Any militancy shown by workers in strikes or labor struggles was certain to be ascribed to the nefarious influence of the omnipresent "Molly Maguires."

On the other hand, there was not yet a wide-spread class-conscious working-class press in the country to counteract the propaganda of the coal operators and to present the Molly Maguires in their true light. The labor paper in which we could find a sustained defense of the Molly Maguires against the nation-wide attack upon them in press and from pulpit was the *Labor Standard* (formerly *The Socialist*), the organ of the Workingman's Party of the

United States, published in New York. In its issue of September 9, 1876, the *Labor Standard* takes up the cudgels against the distortions of the struggle in the anthracite appearing in the capitalist press:

The New York *Herald* like all the other capitalist journals is always ready to attribute "outrages" to the workingmen, and to accuse them with the commission of all kinds of crimes. When a murder is committed in the coal regions the *Herald* without hesitation declares that it was the work of the Molly Maguires. So with fires and other alleged outrages. . . . A *close* investigation might prove that not the Molly Maguires but *paid agents* of the mine owners were the perpetrators of the "outrage." And the *Herald* knows this.

The *Labor Standard's* awareness of the use of "paid agents" and provocateurs by the employers in class struggles shows that the labor movement even of those years had already been confronted with the methods which were to become ready weapons in the employers' arsenal. It is important to note that this class-conscious labor paper, far from shying away from this new challenge in the tactics of class war or being all too ready to accept on face value the fabrications manufactured by these very "paid agents" as was the case with the conservative labor papers of those years and is even more so the case to-day, openly exposed the use of provocateurs by the employers and rose to the defense of the embattled workers.

An editorial in its issue of November 11, 1876, asks: "How long shall the children of toil remain the object of misrepresentation, despotism, the hangman and the wholesale assassin? It is for you, workmen, to answer."

Yet, for fifty years the real nature of this bloody episode has been obscured and distorted by the historians whose chief sources of inspiration have been the writings of F. P.

Dewees, coal company attorney, and Allan Pinkerton, founder of the notorious labor-spy agency, who supplied the mine owners with detectives and provocateurs. Giving free rein to their imagination, these historians have concocted lurid tales about the activities of the Mollies and buried these martyrs of the class struggle deep in the mire of slander and vituperation.

Even among the "labor" historians the Pinkerton description of the Irish miners as "assassins," "incendiaries," "thieves," and "gamblers" is still accepted. Joseph F. Patterson, the last secretary of the miners' Workingmen's Benevolent Association, who because of his activity among the miners during the struggles of the seventies knew the real nature of the struggle, succumbed before the barrage of slander and did not have the courage to defend the miners in the two papers read before the Historical Society of Schuylkill County in 1908 and 1911 on the early organizations of the anthracite miners.[3] This much, however, can be said for him: he could not bring himself to an indorsement of the execution of the Mollies, so he maintained a discreet silence about the whole episode.

This policy is also followed by Chris Evans, former editor of the *United Mine Workers Journal,* who, in his two volumes of labor history published in 1918, does not even mention the conspiracy of the coal operators against the miners.[4]

The questionable virtue of "discreet silence," however, cannot be granted to James Oneal, a leader of the Socialist Party, who in his book, *The Workers in American History,* declares that at least "some of the miners, goaded to desperation by the intolerable conditions, participated in the *criminal acts of the 'Mollies.'* " (Author's Italics.) [5]

In these words we have an acceptance of the coal operators' characterization of the Mollies as a group of desperate criminals who imposed themselves with force and violence upon the miners and induced them to participate in their "criminal acts." The basic class struggle in the anthracite is ignored and the inescapable conclusion is that the Mollies deserved execution.

In contrast to this whole series of falsification and calumny, the words of Eugene V. Debs, written in the *Appeal to Reason* in 1907, for the first time set the whole episode in its true light in one vigorous stroke. Debs declared that the "men who perished upon the scaffold as felons were labor leaders, the first martyrs of the class struggle in the United States." [6] Thus illuminated by one whose class instinct caught the true nature of the struggle, the whole episode should have been carefully studied and made the property of the working class. But the voice of Debs remained buried in the dusty files of the *Appeal to Reason* only to be stifled even more by one who called himself a socialist.

A study of this early struggle reveals Debs to be right and the line of historians from Dewees and Pinkerton to Oneal to be serving the same interests which sent a score of miners to the scaffold. The Mollies were the miners' leaders, at the dawn of a new large-scale industry, in the first major class battle in American labor history.

CHAPTER II

CONDITIONS IN THE ANTHRACITE FIELDS

THE struggle that has come down to us under the fabricated name, the "Molly Maguires," is woven integrally into the warp and woof of nineteenth century America, and was, in particular, an outgrowth of the crisis which shook the country in the decade following the Civil War. The struggle in the Pennsylvania anthracite fields cannot be considered apart from the conditions which created them, and of which they were a part.

When hard coal was first discovered in Pennsylvania by Abijah Smith in 1806 or 1807, the future industrial domain it was to help create was not yet envisaged. Eventually it was to become a great factor in the making of industrial America, but so limited at the time were the needs of incipient capitalism, that in 1814 it was found necessary to mine only twenty-two tons of anthracite.

Developing industries needed more fuel and gradually the problems of mining and transportation were solved. Both industrial and domestic uses were rapidly being found for anthracite; the wastes of eastern Pennsylvania were being rapidly tunneled and "black diamonds" began pouring from the earth.

A great wave of migration swept the region. The rush to eastern Pennsylvania in those years rivaled the rush to California in 1849. Towns and coal patches sprang up everywhere. Anthracite became a source of wealth and power. By 1830, anthracite land was a rich field for

18

speculation. There were some 48,000 people in Lackawanna, Luzerne and Schuylkill Counties at that time (half again as many as there had been ten years before), and they mined half a million tons of coal (400 times as much as had been produced there in 1820). For seventy years, through the period of the Mollies, the expansion continued, as the following table shows:

THE GROWTH OF POPULATION AND PRODUCTION IN THE COUNTIES OF
LACKAWANNA, LUZERNE AND SCHUYLKILL [7]

Year	Population	Per Cent of increase during each decade	Production in tons	Per Cent of increase during each decade
1830	48,123	53.6	500,000	400.0
1840	73,059	51.8	1,000,000	100.0
1850	116,785	59.8	3,500,000	250.0
1860	179,754	53.9	8,500,000	143.0
1870	277,343	54.3	12,500,000	47.0
1880	352,308	27.0	24,800,000	98.4
1890	497,454	41.2	40,000,000	61.3
1900	623,879	25.4	54,000,000	35.0

"The capitalist, the man of enterprise, and the adventurer," says F. P. Dewees in his book, *The Molly Maguires*, "rushed pell-mell to a mountain region theretofore offering but small inducements to the emigrant, all hoping to realize sudden fortunes from a newly discovered source of wealth. Flourishing towns sprang into existence as if by magic, speculation ran wild, fortunes were claimed to have been made in a day, and all the influences affecting a mining region at fever heat were here in full being." [8]

As long as the coal remained underground it was impossible "to realize sudden fortunes from a newly discovered source of wealth." Those who managed to get possession of coal lands and were wealthy enough to hold them and develop them needed labor to build the mines and dig the coal. Even in this early period of "golden opportunity" the vast majority of the newcomers were forced to remain workers and be exploited. As the fevered rush to the mountain regions slackened, life in these regions began to take on definite form. From frontier confusion there emerged the sharp class division between miners and owners which was soon to be expressed in open conflict.

"Scranton, Wilkes-Barre, Mauch Chunk, Pottsville, and Tamaqua," writes Dewees, "are all business centers wherein are located banks, manufacturing establishments, the general offices of railroad and coal companies, large stores, and where, to a great extent, the wealth of the region naturally clusters." They attract "the coal operator and those whose means enable them to retire from business." Other large towns, "to a certain degree partake of the character of business and social centers, but the mining classes, being largely in the majority, regulate and control them." [9]

Ever conscious of the class lines, Dewees places at the bottom of the social scale the many settlements "entirely composed of miners and laborers and those whose business is either directly or indirectly connected with the mines." Many of them were inhabited exclusively by Irish miners, and these, too, are separated into "the good and valuable citizens" (may we not read this as the submissive and meek?) and the "outlaws and desperadoes" (perhaps they had the will to fight against a miserable lot?).[10]

Even to-day, after a half century of bitter and fierce struggle by the miners to obtain improvements in the "patches" and in the pits, many unnecessary and brutal hazards remain; no miner can be reasonably certain when he leaves home for the pit mouth that he will return alive. But in the time of which we write, the horrors of mining were literally indescribable. There were no provisions for safety nor proper ventilation within the pits; mine inspectors were unheard of. The health and lives of the miners were at the mercy of the operators who bitterly opposed every move for protective legislation. Not until 1870 was it required, even theoretically, that mine owners provide such a simple and rudimentary safeguard as a second exit to allow for escape when the main shaft is blocked by explosion, fire, or cave-in.

John L. Sexton, a writer of the period, summed up the attitude of the operators in these words:

So eager were the mine owners to open up their mines that the health and safety of their employees were never taken into consideration. It was coal they wanted and the trifling incident of one, two, or half a dozen of miners in the pits, or more properly "crematories," must not stand in the way of progress and developments. "Accidents will happen," says the mine owner, "in all great works." [11]

On May 6, 1854, the *Daily Miners' Journal*, a mine owners' paper in Pottsville, published a letter, typical of many others, from one John Morris, "The coal operators do not take the necessary precautions for the safety of the miners that are required," he wrote. "Cases prevail to a great extent in the mining districts of this county and the coal operators in many instances have not sufficient ventilation to clean the mines well. What can you as miners do? Can you not get your representatives at Harrisburg to appoint competent men as inspectors of mines to see that there is proper ventilation and men's lives are not trifled with for the sake of a little gain?"

But the state legislature then—as now—was under the influence of the coal operators; only vigorous mass action could force it to concede even the slightest reforms. The mass meetings, resolutions and petitions addressed to it by the workers, demanding protective legislation, were altogether ineffectual because not yet sufficiently powerful.

The great Avondale fire of September 6, 1869, which took a toll of 179 miners' lives, turned the tables for a time. The mine caught fire from the furnace at the bottom of the shaft which was at one time the only airway and the single entrance to the pit. Here men were caught and roasted like so many helpless fowl. The anthracite miners were roused as they had never been before. They exerted pressure too great to be resisted and the legislature, with great reluctance, passed laws stipulating, for Schuylkill County only, second openings for mines, forced ventilation and the appointment of a state mine inspector.

This by no means signified a real victory. The laws, as passed, were still weak. Provisions for their enforcement, in some cases altogether lacking, were often nullified by the courts.

Mine inspectors, political appointees, were often under the complete domination of the operators whose position of economic control gave them legal and governmental dominance as well. And even when the inspector was vigorous, his protest was usually buried with his report in the neglected archives of the state.

The report of Frank Schmeltzer, a mine inspector for the Pottsville district, for instance, is a record of disregarded safety laws, calmly continued over the inspector's protest.

"I served notices on the Ravensdale Colliery," he notes, "requiring them to comply with instructions for necessary improvement as regards safe let-out, proper ventilation of the mine, and keeping in order the needed repairs, requiring new slope rope and the security of the drum gear. . . . By a severe explosion Mr. Moss, one of the operators, with others, lost his life; *hence the necessity exists to enforce obedience to the law.*" (Author's italics.)

At the Saint Clair Shaft and Live Oak Collieries there was insufficient air for safety; and at the latter, "a large amount of explosive gas generated."

"On several occasions," Schmeltzer had "officially visited the [Beachwood] colliery, and also at the request of several complainants, whose statements were found to be substantially correct. . . . This firm used two wagons at a time and permitted as many persons to ascend and descend at a time as pleased to do so, thus jeopardizing the lives of the whole. While several accidents occurred, yet these acts, in contravention of the law, were not as yet abated. The posting of notices and our remonstrances were rejected and proved of no avail."

And as for the Eagle Shaft Colliery, there were, "but fair promises which were never intended to be fulfilled." The owners "set the law at defiance."

The mine inspector, "after repeated remonstrances made to . . . [the Norwegian Colliery] for the necessary relief to their miners, and a compliance with the requirements of the law, for a proper ventilation of their mines and the safety and health of their miners" was, he wrote, "forced to apply for an injunction which would restrain their employment of men for the purpose of working in this most dangerous mine."

He noted, too, that "needed instruction for repairs and proper drainage had been given, and for a safe outlet for miners in case of danger, to escape by." But: "Little or no effort has been made to comply with my instructions."

"Visits to this colliery," he added sadly, "are frequent, but of little relief so far, while legal decision is pending." [12]

Nor was relief so easily forthcoming, as this inspector would soon discover. The Court of Common Pleas of Luzerne County refused to restrain the operation of this mine without a second opening, on the ground that the law in question referred only to mines "worked through a shaft or slope," while this particular pit was operated through a tunnel.

Just what difference it made to a miner burning at the colliery was not discussed by the learned judge. And there were certainly many miners who did burn, or who were crushed, or maimed and injured in a dozen ways, most of them preventable. In Schuylkill County 566 miners were killed and 1,665 maimed in seven years; in 1871 alone, 112 were killed and 339 permanently injured. Page after page from the reports of those who visited the pits reveal them as literal death traps. In a report to the governor of Pennsylvania, P. F. M'Andrew, clerk of the mining district of Schuylkill wrote: "The lists of casualties hereto subjoined fully demonstrate the havoc on life and limb, occasioned by bad ventilation and a negligence in not removing these deleterious elements, beside the great misery it ever afterwards entails upon the widows and orphans of our mining communities."

Again in 1875, he wrote: "The employees in coal mines are handled so as their labor shall realize the largest amount of profit to the employer, and this at the risk of life and limb, consequent upon diversity of their labor, besides the danger to be encountered in working in deep mines that are so often idle that, from standing gas, decay of timber, the absence of ventilation, and standing water, not only makes the mine unsafe but virtually dangerous." And: "The miner's occupation in some cases is but little better than semi-slavery." [13]

Yet only six years after the great Avondale fire, the mine owners whittled down whatever reforms had been won by the miners in struggle. The mine inspector's office became formal, even decorative. Except where reënforced by the belligerence of workers at the individual pits it accomplished little. The operators and politicians used it as a pretext to block any real reform. But this severe oppression was molding a struggle that would take form in the great strike of 1875—a struggle which resulted but did not end with the execution, as Molly Maguires, of a score of militant miners' leaders.

The "bob-tailed check," miserably low wages and the resulting low standard of living were equally active in bringing about the militant mass effort of the miners to improve their conditions. In 1839 a miner received one dollar a day, a laborer about eighty-two cents. Ten years later the miner's wage had increased by a quarter of a dollar, and the laborer's by a cent or so.* But in 1850 they had dropped again. The skilled man received eighty or ninety cents, the unskilled sixty or sixty-five cents. This table, reproduced from Dr. Peter Roberts' *The Anthracite Coal Industry,* shows the actual wages paid by one company during the forties:

Year	Miner per day	Laborer per day
1839	$1.00	$.82
1840	$1.00	.80
1842	.87	.70
1844	1.10	.76
1845	1.13	.80
1846	1.25	.83
1847	1.25	.83
1848	1.25	.83

"These were low wages," says Dr. Roberts, "but they were actually lower than the amounts specified, for the men were not paid in money. They had to take their earnings out in goods, which made a difference of 15 to 20 per cent

* The average mine wage in the Harlan County, Kentucky, coal fields in 1931 was about $30.00 a *month.*

against the wage earners." [14]   He shows a table of prices, covering eighteen commodities in company and town stores. On every item the company price is from 10 to 50 per cent higher. Sixteen instead of twenty bars of soap for a dollar; sixty instead of forty cents for a bushel of corn, and seventy instead of sixty cents for the same quantity of potatoes; eight instead of five cents for a yard of calico.*

The company stores were a source of bitterness almost from the first years of the industry—an abuse that still remains in the coal areas. They were an important factor in the strike of 1849, and in the seventies the Workingmen's Benevolent Association, the miners' union, opposed them as a system of robbery.

Sometimes wages were not paid at all. Many companies, finding themselves in financial difficulties, reorganized and transferred their assets to new corporations owned by the same men; the miners were left to hold a large corner of the bag. In the middle of the century a mass protest was fermenting among the mine workers, which was to break into the first great coal miners' strike. On January 13, 1849, there was a great mass meeting at Pottsville to formulate plans of action.

"Shall the workingmen of Pennsylvania lay supinely on their backs and bear all the burdens heaped upon them by those who have desires to make princely fortunes out of labor and toil," the resolution asked, "or shall we arise in our strength and cast aside the bonds which have been thrown about us by demagogues and gamesters? . . . We ask no favors from nabobs, lordlings or capitalists. Our rights are our own; we are determined to have them." [15]

Four months later thousands of unorganized miners

---

* These prices were secured in community studies made just before 1900 and probably refer specifically to the later nineties. But the grievance dates back to the earlier days.

downed tools, moved by their own misery and a growing sense of their need and power to "arise in strength." The demand was for wages paid in money. The miners would "insist upon monthly settlements and payments for miners and laborers and that all payments be made in money, as no store orders will be received hereafter." And finally, in 1876, a bill was introduced which provided that coal companies must pay their workers in cash. The operators objected out of the usual solicitude for the liberties of the miners and because "it took certain means of income from the coal operators and gave them to the merchants."

But what the passage of such a law would mean to the operators is aptly illustrated by an order introduced into the lower house of the Pennsylvania legislature, having been sent by one of the coal companies to its workers:

You will, therefore, please understand, one and all, that from this time henceforth we shall take particular notice of who deals at the store and who does not. And as the time is near at hand when we shall reduce the number of our men, just such men as have no account at the store will be dropped, and those who have shown the sense to deal justly will be retained at work so long as it is in our power to keep them. After the spring run is over, and the dry season sets in, it is our purpose to employ from 40 to 50 men at each works, and they will be most certainly selected in the manner we have above noted. We have started this store for our mutual benefit, and we intend to run it; and although our people have not given it that support due from them after a fair, honest trial, we are now determined that it must be done, and that the store shall receive the patronage of all our employees without exception—not through any force or compulsory measure on our part, but only by keeping such men as do so of their own free will.

(Signed) JOSEPH WALTON Co.[16]

And thus the miners "of their own free will" and without "any force or compulsory measure"—except, of course, the

mere threat of losing their job—were forced to partake of
the benefits of the company stores and the "bob-tailed
check."

The miners were continuing their struggle in the pits and
in the legislature. Just as the operators tried to block the
organization of the miners by sending their leaders to the
gallows, they blocked every effort at legislative reform, no
matter how meek, by every means at their disposal.

The major struggle was postponed for a time by the
Civil War, which increased both the demand and price of
coal. Coal which sold at $3.20 a ton in 1859 brought $8.59
in 1864. Labor, too, was scarce and in the midst of high
prices and even higher profits the workers secured an advance in pay.

But with the end of war, inevitable deflation began. The
bottom fell out of the coal market and two wage cuts hit
the miners in quick succession. By 1867 they were getting
one-fourth less than three years before, while the general
price level had dropped hardly a tenth. Then the coal
market recovered and wages were pushed up for a time.
According to Dr. Roberts, 1869, *the year of the highest
wage*, brought an average of $18.20 a week. This was fol-
lowed by a series of cuts which extended in rapid succession
through the following years. By 1877, when the miners'
organization was already destroyed, and the first group of
miner-militants were being hanged as Molly Maguires, the
average had dropped to $9.80—lower than it had been since
the first year of the Civil War.

Often, when tools, supplies, food and rent were deducted
from earnings—for the miner's house, like his food, was had
from the company—there was nothing (or less than that) to
show. The "bob-tailed check" became a commonality in
the miner's life and passed into his idiom: it was a slip of
paper, worth nothing, and indicating merely that all his

earnings had passed back to the company. The following example is taken from a period somewhat later, 1896, when wages were higher but it illustrates what the system meant: [17]

Coal mined, 49 tons at 71½ cents		$35.03
Supplies	$8.25	
Blacksmith	.30	
Fixing two drills	.30	
Rent	6.00	
Groceries, etc.	20.18	
Total		35.03
Net Balance		$00.00

It was not until 1881 that a law was passed to enforce the payment of wages in money, but only to be declared unconstitutional. The law was, the court said, "an infringement alike of the right of the employer and employee; more than this, it is an insulting attempt to put the laborer under legislative tutelage, which is not only degrading to his manhood, but subversive of his rights as a citizen of the United States." [18]

Bitter was the miner's life. In his sayings and songs he cursed it:

There's one thing I'll tell you and don't you forget
That your back with the droppers is all wringing wet,
Your clothes they are soaking; your shoes are wet through,
Oh! never be a miner whatever you do.

Or he would sing:

I'm getting old and feeble and I can work no more;
I have laid the rusty mining tools away—
For forty years and over I have toiled about the mines,
But now I'm getting feeble, old and gray.

I started on the breaker and went back to it again,
But now my work is finished for all time;
The only place that's left me is the almshouse for a home,
That's where I'll lay this weary head of mine.[19]

The breaker—where the vari-sized lumps of coal, as they come from the pits, pass on belts to be broken and graded—is the first place at which young boys are put to work; and many old men who can no longer work hard and fast enough to hold a place below, return to it.

A vivid description of the exploitation under which the child workers suffered is given by the correspondent of the *Labor Standard* (May 17, 1877) who visited the mines in the anthracite. His description of the breaker room in the Hickory Colliery, near St. Clair, Pa., is worth quoting in full:

In these works 300 men and boys are employed; and when I went through the buildings and through the mine I saw them all. Among all these 300, although I was with them for hours, I did not hear a laugh or even see a smile.

In a little room in this big, black shed—a room not twenty feet square—where a broken stove, red-hot, tries vainly to warm the cold air that comes in through the open window, forty boys are picking their lives away. The floor of the room is an inclined plane, and a stream of coal pours constantly in from some unseen place above, crosses the room, and pours out again into some unseen place below. Rough board seats stretch across the room, five or six rows of them, very low and very dirty, and on these the boys sit, and separate the slate from the coal as it runs down the inclined plane. It is a painful sight to see the men going so silently and gloomily about their work, but it is a thousand times worse to see these boys. They work here, in this little black hole, all day and every day, trying to keep cool in summer, trying to keep warm in winter, picking away among the black coals, bending over till their little spines are curved, never saying a word all the live-long day.

I stood and watched these boys for a long time, without being seen by them, for their backs are turned toward the entrance door and the coal makes such a racket that they cannot hear anything a foot from their ears. They were muffled up in old coats and old shawls and old scarfs, and ragged mittens to keep their hands from freezing, and as they sat and picked and picked, gathering little heaps of blackened slate by their sides, they looked more like so many black dwarfs than like a party of fresh young boys. The air was cold enough and the work was lively enough to paint any boy's cheeks in rosy colors; but if there was a red cheek in the room it was well hidden under the coating of black dust that covered everything. These little fellows go to work in this cold, dreary room at seven o'clock in the morning and work till it is too dark to see any longer. For this they get from $1 to $3 a week. One result of their work is the clean, free coal, that burns away to ashes in the grate; another result I found in a little miners' graveyard, beside a pretty little church, where more than every other stone bears the name of some little fellow under fifteen years of age.

The boys are all sizes and ages, from little fellows scarce big enough to be wearing pantaloons up to youths of fifteen and sixteen. After they reach this age they go to work in the mine, for there they can make more money. Not three boys in all this roomful could read or write. Shut in from everything that is pleasant, with no chance to learn, with no knowledge of what is going on about them, with nothing to do but work, grinding their little lives away in this dusty room, they are no more than the wire screens that separate the great lumps of coal from the small. They have no games; when their day's work is done they are too tired for that. They know nothing but the difference between slate and coal.

The smallest of the boys do not get more than $1 a week, and from this the pay goes up to $2 and $3. Some of them live several miles from the colliery, and are carried to the mine every morning in the cars and back again every night, the company charging them ten cents for each trip and deducting the fares from their wages at the end of the month. Sometimes, after the boys have got to the mine, they find that some accident has stopped the work; then they have nothing to do for the day and get no pay. In this way, I am told, it is no unusual thing for a boy to find, at the end of the month, that his indebtedness to the company for railroad fares is some dollars more than the company's indebtedness to him for labor; so that he has worked all the month for a few dollars less than nothing.

Even now child labor is not uncommon in the United States; then no boy was too young to go onto the breaker. As soon as he was physically able to perform the task, regardless of the cost to his body and mind, he went to the mine every morning with his father whose own twelve or fourteen hours of labor could not support the family.

For example, in Schuylkill County alone out of 22,000 miners in 1870, 5,500 were boys between the ages of seven and sixteen. In one of the early poems a miner complains:

> In the chutes I graduated instead of going to school—
> Remember, friends, my parents they were poor;
> When a boy left the cradle it was always made the rule
> To try to keep starvation from the door.
> At eight years of age to the breaker first I went,
> To learn the occupation of a slave.

While the miner crawled underground in mud and water, breathing coal dust and powder smoke, emerging from the living hell below—if not blasted to death or mutilated—only to find his rest in hovels unfit for habitation, the mine owners and the investors in coal companies were reaping enormous profits. And lower on the scale of profits than the owners were the mine boss and superintendent, to the workers the most immediate and visible oppressors.

The mine bosses were usually workers taken out of the ranks. They were given a fairly high wage and no manual work was required of them. They also had, and exerted, the privilege of petty graft at the expense of those who worked under them—they sold jobs and collected bribes for keeping them. They were responsible to mine superintendents. They were the tools with which the great tyrannies were carried out. They became spies for the owners: they did the actual job—always dictated from above—of short weighing, of increasing profits at the expense of the miners and mercilessly crushing protest.

The mine managers and superintendents, who stood above the bosses, were the representatives of absentee owners at the mines. They were well paid and comfortably off—so long as their operations produced profits. They dared not indulge in sympathy for the miners. "Corporations have no souls," said *Harper's Weekly* editorially on September 25, 1869, "and managers and superintendents must spend little and make much or they are in danger of losing their place."

By the seventies wealthy financiers were already in control of the leading anthracite companies. Railroads carrying coal saw the possibilities for profits at every stage, from the digging at the coal face to the final delivery at the furnace bin. The Philadelphia and Reading Railroad was a pioneer in that field and had staked out claims with an eye toward a monopoly in Schuylkill County. It was to achieve that end that Franklin B. Gowen, its president in the seventies, took a leading rôle in smashing the miners' union and became State prosecutor against its most militant leaders when they were tried and condemned to death as Molly Maguires. When the coal subsidiary of the Reading was organized in 1871, the railroad had already acquired some 70,000 acres of land, and its annual report said:

"The result of this action has been to secure and attach to the company's railroad a body of coal lands capable of supplying all the coal tonnage that can possibly be transported over the road for centuries." [20]

According to Dr. Roberts: "In 1870, 75 per cent of all the collieries in this district had passed into the hands of the Reading Railroad." Five years later its holdings had been increased still further. Only the organized resistance of the miners could limit the tyranny exercised by such corporations.

The origin of most of the important American capitalist fortunes can be traced to the Civil War and the period immediately following it. The bases for such powerful interests as steel, railroads, banking and oil were laid during this struggle. The Civil War finally established the supremacy of the capitalist class in America. While tens of thousands of workers and poor farmers were dying at the front to save the Union and destroy chattel slavery, the northern capitalists were busily building their fortunes. At the war's end they were masters of the country. The southern slaveowner was eliminated from Congress; the so-called free trade doctrine was forgotten; Congress raised the average of tariff rates "from about nineteen per cent as fixed by the measure of 1857 to forty-seven per cent in the law of 1864." [21] The effect on industry, including coal, was tremendous. The shortage of labor, the increased demand due to the war, and the continuous migration from East to West, afforded the workers an opportunity to win higher wages and improved working conditions.

Congress came to the aid of the industrial capitalists with an extraordinary law, the Immigration Act of 1864, which gave federal authorization to the importation of workers under the terms of contracts analogous to those of the indentured servants of colonial times.[22] In practice this meant a return to bond-slavery for the white workingman in America.

The device was a success. The stream of immigration

swelled, within a few years carrying between two and three million workers to this country. They poured into the mills and mines to do the hardest and lowest paid work. At the same time they composed a tremendous reserve of labor which the capitalists could use to beat down still further the standard of living of the American working class and combat the tendency among the workers to struggle for better conditions.

The closing of the war saw a dawning period of prosperity for those who owned the country's wealth of industry. The railroads were stretching across wide spaces which were rapidly being filled by the restless westward movement of those who thought they would thus obtain release from the misery, poverty and exploitation under which they chafed. Hundreds of millions of dollars poured into industrial enterprises. Fat war contracts had been pocketed by manufacturers and jobbers. The system of war finance—funds obtained by floating loans through the banks, rather than by taxation of the vast war profits—gave banking houses enormous wealth and power. During the entire conflict the sum of all tax collections was only $667,000,000; government borrowing during the period bulked to $2,261,000,000. In the four years of the war the national debt rose from $74,985,000 to $2,846,000,000.[23]

Simultaneously with this increase in capitalists' fortunes there was a growth of the movement for an eight-hour day among the workers of the country. On August 20, 1866, the delegates of sixty labor unions gathered in Baltimore to found the National Labor Union and passed a resolution which declared that:

The first and great necessity at the present, to free labor of this country from capitalist slavery, is the passing of a law by which eight hours shall be the normal working day in all states in the

American union. We are resolved to put forth all our strength until this glorious result is attained.

Under the terms of the child-labor act of 1848, Pennsylvania already had a ten-hour workday for the employees of certain types of factories. Now, in 1866, almost simultaneously with the passage of the National Labor Union's founding resolution, an eight-hour bill was introduced into the Pennsylvania legislature. At first miners were not included under its terms, but during the discussion an amendment was adopted which included them. Shortly after, a second amendment was added, negating the law in cases where agreements upon hours of labor existed between the individual employer and his workers; and in this form the bill was finally passed. But in this form, of course, it had no meaning—any employer could make a work-period agreement a condition of employment and so evade it.

The eight-hour day sentiment became wide-spread and it gained the support of the masses. Several other state legislatures were forced to pass the eight-hour law. However, these laws were never intended to be put into force. "For all practical intents and purposes," declared the committee on the eight-hour day at the second convention of the National Labor Union, "they might as well have never been placed on the statute books, and can only be described as frauds on the laboring class." [24]

In 1868, nearly 20,000 anthracite miners struck for an eight-hour day. They remained on strike four months before being forced back without making any gain. A year later they were organized into a number of county unions, the most powerful of which was the Workingmen's Benevolent Association of Schuylkill County, led by John Siney. The W. B. A. again declared a strike. It had accepted the condition of a sliding wage scale, depending on the price of coal, but it demanded also a minimum below which wages would not be allowed to fall.

The miners were now fighting "the notorious Franklin B. Gowen." [25]   This struggle was to develop in the very near future into the first major life and death struggle between the first of the coal trusts and the miners in which at least nineteen anthracite miners were to die on the scaffold as Molly Maguires.

Nor was the struggle restricted merely to eastern Pennsylvania. It was part of a nation-wide conflict taking place during the seventies and eighties. The period of expansion after the Civil War had ended with a crisis. A merry orgy of speculation turned to one of the bitterest economic crises in the history of the country at the dawn of the era of American imperialism—just as another, with deeper and sharper consequences, would in 1929-32, when Wall Street imperialism was already beginning to ebb. As at the later date, the capitalists attempted to shift the whole weight of the crisis upon the working class. Unemployment was widespread. Over three million workers—a vast proportion of the population of the time—were thrown out of work in 1873. Whole families perished daily of starvation.

The unions which had grown up, not only in the mine districts but throughout the country in the sixties, were bitterly attacked. In the railway strike of 1877, Federal troops were called into a labor struggle for the first time, and the courts defined a labor union as a "malicious conspiracy."

Workers refused to accept the burden of depression without resistance. In the anthracite fields, in every industrial area, there were bitter strikes, gigantic demonstrations, bloody clashes with police. In the period of prosperity and expansion the trade union movement had made considerable progress; by the time the war ended local trade unions and national organizations had been established in most of the basic industries. The National Labor Union had been organized; and, in many industrial centers, there were revolutionary sections of the First International. The struggle of the Paris workers and the establishment of the Commune in 1871 had its reverberations in the United States. The American working class was not altogether unprepared to meet the attacks of the employers against wages, living standards and the trade union organizations.

In 1875 the anthracite miners again went on strike, their strike coinciding with the numerous bitter struggles of the textile workers in the same year.

On June 21, 1877, the miners' leaders were hanged at Pottsville and Mauch Chunk, and on the seventeenth day of the next month began the long and bitter general strike of railroad workers against a wage reduction. In Pittsburgh alone, twenty-six strikers were slaughtered by the armed forces of the state; in Reading thirteen more were killed; and many others lost their lives in other railroad centers.

The events in the anthracite regions in the sixties and the seventies were a link in the chain of such events throughout the United States. The bloody attack on the miners, their defeat and the destruction of their organizations, heralded a crushing blow to workers in other industries.

CHAPTER III

EARLY ORGANIZATIONS OF THE ANTHRACITE MINERS

ABOUT fifteen hundred miners downed tools on July 8, 1842, in the first anthracite strike of which record has come down to us. "They were joined by many idle and vicious men," we read in the *History of Schuylkill County, Pa.*, "and they forcibly prevented others, who were disposed to do so, from pursuing their labor. Some riots ensued, but the authorities acted promptly, order was restored, and work was resumed in two or three weeks." [26] Thus the first serious attempt of the anthracite miners to better their conditions was effectively smashed and "order was restored" by the operators and the government.

The first actual organization appeared seven years later. John Bates of St. Clair was the leader of the miners of Schuylkill County during this early period, and in 1849 he organized a local group commonly referred to as the Bates Union. The *Daily Miners' Journal,* published at Pottsville as an organ of the coal owners, in its issue of May 5, 1849, tells about a mass meeting held at Minersville on May 2 and attended by over 2,000 miners. In a long resolution the miners set forth their grievances and declared: "We desire to impress upon the miners and laborers of Schuylkill County the importance of unanimous, firm, determined, but at the same time mild and respectful action and we recommend the formation of a *miners' union.*"

The resolution further suggested definite measures for

uniting the forces of the workers: "We recommend the appointment of a committee of two from each colliery to form a central committee to make the necessary arrangements for the formation of a miners' union, if they shall deem it necessary, and also to negotiate with employers." [27]

The Bates Union existed only a short time. It led a strike in 1849 against payment of wages in script but in the fall of 1850 it disintegrated. Bates was accused by the miners of betraying their interests and secretly selling them out to the coal operators—a charge that was to be repeated often in the future as members of the United Mine Workers of America fought against their misleaders. Bates himself disappeared with the funds of the organization.[28]

It is interesting to note that most of the leaders of the miners at the time, such as John Bates, Thomas Lloyd, Daniel Weaver, John Siney, were English, Welsh and Irish immigrants who had taken part in the Chartist movement. All of them had a militant background for the struggle in America.

The early efforts of the miners to better their conditions by organizing took the form of local unions and benevolent societies, organized primarily to assist their members during sickness. Thus *The Constitution and By-Laws of the Miners' Benevolent Society of Pittston, Luzerne Co., Pa.*, set forth its aim as follows: "In order that the stranger may find the kind attention and fostering care of a brother when sick, and be encouraged in resolutions of morality and sobriety at all times, we, citizens . . . have formed ourselves into a Benevolent Society and body politic in law. . . ." Habitual drunkards, gamblers and criminals were excluded from this society.

Such societies and local unions became centers of hope and inspiration to the miners, anthracite as well as bituminous. Through them the miners learned the value of collective action and the importance of organization. Soon they discovered that their strength lay in their organized efforts. As the class struggle became sharper in the coal fields, some of these benevolent societies even acquired the character of trade unions.

But the small operators began to give way to the bigger operators and coal companies. The power of the employers increased. The local organizations of the miners found they could not make an effective fight by acting separately. From bitter experience the miners learned the necessity of a national organization embracing both anthracite and bituminous fields. In 1860, therefore, a call appeared for a national miners' union. It was signed by Daniel Weaver, a soft coal miner of Illinois, and ended with this stirring appeal:

Come, then, and rally around the standard of union—the union of states and the unity of miners—and with honesty of purpose, zeal and watchfulness, the pledge of success, unite for the emancipation of our labor and the regeneration and elevation, physically, mentally and morally, of our species.[29]

At the convention which followed on January 28, 1861, at St. Louis, Missouri, the American Miners' Association was organized. The miners' urge for united struggle against exploitation is shown by the following verses which they used as an introduction to their new constitution:

> Step by step the longest march
>   Can be won, can be won;
> Single stones will form an arch
>   One by one, one by one.
>
> And by union, what we will,
>   Can be all accomplished still,
> Drops of water turn a mill,
>   Singly none, singly none.

The American Miners' Association grew very rapidly, but it was never more than a loosely knit federation of local bodies and by 1868 it had lost its influence and gradually dwindled away. Local efforts at organization continued, however. In 1864, the Workingmen's Benevolent Society of Carbon County, Pa., was formed, and in 1868 the local societies of the southern district were united in the Workingmen's Benevolent Association of Schuylkill County. John Siney, a recent Irish immigrant who had worked in the English coal mines, was elected president.

In his declaration, December 2, 1868, Siney stated the aims of the Schuylkill County association as follows:

The object of the W. B. A. is to unite in one band of brotherhood all who earn their bread by hard toil—more especially the miners and laborers of Pennsylvania. Benevolence is not sectional, but willingly assists all who need assistance. But, before we can assist one another we must become united, so that, to whatever locality the miner may move, he will find a home and friends to take care of him. . . .

Our eyes are being opened and we look back to our folly for not sooner uniting ourselves for our mutual benefit.

Without obligations, signs or password, we move along, fearless of impostors, and determined to judge for ourselves in the future, having clearly learned that our labor is our own capital, that our company is a strong one, and that its stock is always worth its par value.

The leadership of the Association was opposed to the militant policy from the very start. They wanted the miners' organization to remain "respectable." In the same declaration Siney complains bitterly against the editor of the *Scranton Morning Republican* who judged the miners by "something he has read, in times gone by about 'Molly McGuires,' 'Buckshots,' etc." Siney was for "law and order." "By the rules of the association," he declared, "all acts of violence are strictly forbidden, and any member found guilty of such act will not only be expelled from the association, but from the county also, and we hope soon to say, from the six anthracite counties, for where our laws go they will carry with them strict adherence to social law and order." [30] The leadership went into the struggle only when and where it could no longer withstand the pressure of the militant rank and file.

In June of the same year, 20,000 miners throughout the anthracite struck for the eight-hour day, but the struggle which lasted until September proved to be unsuccessful. The following spring the W. B. A. in Schuylkill County and similar organizations in the other anthracite districts called another strike. The price of coal was falling and the miners knew that this would mean a fresh cut in their wages. The leaders called a strike in order to reduce the stocks of coal which were piling up. They accepted the principle of the sliding scale of wages, varying as the price of coal went up or down, but they demanded a minimum base below which the wage rate should not be allowed to fall. A few operators offered an immediate increase and their miners remained at work. But in general the strike revealed a strong, loyal solidarity. Officially, the strike was called off after four weeks, but the last miners did not return to work until the end of August. They had not secured the basic minimum wage.

This strike awoke the fury and fear of the operators; they denounced it as "criminal" and "outrageous." The capitalist press was filled with threats against the strikers and "agitators." But a few months later the operators entered into the negotiations with Siney and the other officials of the miners, and on July 29, 1870, the first joint agreement was signed by representatives of the operators and officers of the Workingmen's Benevolent Association.

The agreement fixed the details of the sliding wage scale. It provided also "that the Workingmen's Benevolent Association shall not sustain any man who is discharged for incompetency, bad workmanship, bad conduct, or other good cause; and that the operators shall not discharge any man or officer for actions or duties imposed on him by the Workingmen's Benevolent Association." [31]   In the same year, 1870, the name of the association was changed to the Miners' and Laborers' Association, but the old initials, W. B. A., continued in popular everyday use.

On the basis of this sliding scale, wages fell as the price of coal went down. In January, 1871, a strike against wage cuts began in the northern anthracite district and spread into Schuylkill County. The men were out for several months until Siney and others persuaded the miners to accept an umpire's compromise award. But this time no union agreement was signed and the operators refused to deal with the W. B. A.

The W. B. A., however, was growing in numbers and influence among the anthracite miners who rallied to it as the only possible means of improving their conditions. The operators, on the other hand, were determined to destroy it and reëstablish complete autocratic power over their employees. Dewees pictures the situation thus:

It is natural for man to avail himself of power, and the power of labor was in the ascendant. Encroachment after encroachment was made upon the rights of the employer, until it came to be claimed that no man should be employed and no man discharged except as sanctioned by the "Union." The manner of working, the hours of working, the superintendents and the bosses, were held to be under their control and subject to their direction. They claimed a right to fix a rate of wages and time of payment, without at the same time according to the employer the privilege of refusing their demands and employing others in their stead. Some of these acts are attributable to the circumstances which gave them the power, and others to the pernicious influence of the band of criminals who foisted themselves among them.

This "band of criminals" committed the unpardonable offense of establishing union control of the job. And who were these "criminals"? Dewees tells us:

Whilst it is an act of simple justice to the leaders of the "Labor Union" to acknowledge that, as a general rule, the true interests of the workingmen, from their standpoint, were sought to be obtained peaceably and through compromise, and whilst in such efforts they had the approval of the great body of the society, unreasonable demands were pressed through the influence and granted through fear of the Molly Maguires.[82]

The Schuylkill County W. B. A. was one of the local union bodies which joined in a call for a new national union of miners. The second national miners' convention took place at Youngstown, Ohio, on October 13, 1873, with delegates in attendance from Illinois, West Virginia, Ohio, Pennsylvania, and Indiana. It organized the Miners' National Association of the United States of America and elected John Siney as president. Arbitration and agreements were put forward as more desirable than strikes, but even so non-militant an organization met with aggressive hostility from the operators in all the coal fields. In four years this national union also had disintegrated and disappeared.

Siney's withdrawal from the W. B. A. to take the presidency of the Miners' National Association in 1873 did not apparently change the situation in Schuylkill County, where a sharp conflict was in progress between vacillating and timid officials who stood for compromise, and rank and file miners who were for vigorous strikes.

Besides the W. B. A., which included miners of all nationalities, the Irish miners had their semi-secret organization, the Ancient Order of Hibernians.

The A. O. H. in America was an extension of the organization of the same name in Ireland. There, the organization was strictly secret. Thomas Frances McGrath, in his *History of the Ancient Order of Hibernians,* would have us believe that the sole aim and object of the organization was to protect the Catholic Church and its priests from the English government. Undoubtedly this was one of its objects. But as the time went on, it became more and more an expression of the resistance of the Irish peasants against the English landlords who robbed them of their lands by force and exploited and oppressed them.

The American miners of Irish descent were the first to band together under the same old banner of the A. O. H., which, in the preamble of its constitution, stated its aims as follows:

The members of this order do declare that the intent and purpose of the Order is to promote FRIENDSHIP, UNITY and TRUE CHRISTIAN CHARITY among its members, by raising and supporting a stock or fund of money for maintaining the aged, sick, blind, and infirm members, and for no other purpose whatsoever.

UNITY, in uniting together for mutual support in sickness and distress.

FRIENDSHIP, in assisting each other to the best of our power.

TRUE CHRISTIAN CHARITY, by doing to each other, and all the world, as we would wish them to do unto us.

And the American by-laws specifically stated:

SEC. 10. If any member of this order be convicted of robbery, perjury, or any other atrocious offense, he shall be excluded from the Order for life.

The general aims as proposed here did not, however, stand in the way of the anthracite miners when they transformed the benevolent organization into an organ of struggle against the operators, even those of Irish descent, when the occasion demanded. Here we need only state that the operators could not crush the miners' union completely as long as its very backbone, the A. O. H., remained alive and militant.

The president of the A. O. H. in America, Mathew Cummings, has the following to say about its origin:

The organization has been known in the old land [Ireland] by different names—Confederationists, Whiteboys, and Ribbonmen, and at last became known as the Hibernian Society, as the name of Ribbonmen had been outlawed by the English government. It was afterwards called St. Patrick's Fraternal Society. Then it was named the Ancient Order of Hibernians.[33]

When Irish immigrants and miners of Irish descent in the anthracite entered into a life and death struggle they found that they were in conflict with coal corporations in which British capital was heavily invested. The age-old struggle between English landlords and capitalists and Irish workers and peasants was, to a degree, reflected, under new conditions and changed circumstances, in the struggle in the coal fields. The living traditions of struggle of the Whiteboys and Ribbonmen were carried over in the A. O. H. and lived again in the struggles of the anthracite miners. Centuries of history through which the Irish masses, battered by oppression and scourged by famine, had struggled, formed a background of stubborn resistance and determined struggle for the Irish miners in the anthracite.

Their people had suffered through Cromwell's conquest of 1649-1653 and the subjugation of the country under the yoke of British imperialism. The communal and tribal ownership of land which was the basis of Irish society was completely and brutally transformed when the British conquerors began their methodical destruction in 1650.

So complete was this violent expropriation of the peasants' land, that after the Cromwellian War, only 800,000 acres "were left in the hands of the old Irish." The Irish peasants became tenants, virtual serfs, harboring a deep and bitter resentment toward their conquerors.

On the heels of the famine of 1740, when hundreds of thousands of the poor perished from hunger, the cattle pestilence in England led the ruling class to lift the embargo on Irish cattle and cattle products, and the transformation of the farm lands of Ireland into great pastures was begun. Tenants, driven from the land, were left to die of hunger and exposure. Even those who retained a hold on the land could not wring from it both a living for themselves and the extravagant demands of the landlords.

The Irish poor, driven to desperation, revolted; secret societies sprung up all over the country. Deprived of the land they tilled and, thereby, of their only means of livelihood, they fought for the very right to existence, tearing down inclosures, digging up fields and rendering them useless as pasture lands, burning the houses of the shepherds. Although it is impossible to tell whether the rebellious peasants had any coherent organization, they were called Whiteboys in the South—"from the practice of wearing white shirts over their clothes when on nocturnal expeditions" [34]—and Oakboys and Hearts of Steelboys in the North. But their aim was the same everywhere. Drawn together by common suffering from a common cause, they challenged the arrogant landlord class, which mercilessly crushed every sign of resistance among the peasantry. The homes even of the least suspected peasants were raided by night and the inhabitants shot or hanged.

Though Catholicism was hated by the ruling class of England, yet it was hated only to the degree that it was embraced by the great masses of the Irish poor. The English Protestant tyrant had no quarrel with the Catholic "gentlemen" of Ireland. And the Catholic landlord was quite willing to help in the suppression of the Catholic rebel. The high dignitaries of the Church gave all possible assistance to the government in its war upon the poor peasants. They termed the rebel peasants "a gang of wretches" and "deluded victims of the devil," and excommunicated them from the church.[35]

Not only the peasants and agrarian workers, but also the city workers took up the struggle against the foreign oppressors. Under the name of Volunteer Corps, fighting organizations were formed in the cities. James Connolly, the Irish revolutionary leader, tells us that in Dublin "there were three divisions of volunteers . . . the Liberty Corps, recruited exclusively from the working class; the Merchant Corps, composed of the capitalist class, and the Lawyers Corps." [36]

The Society of United Irishmen formed secretly in 1791 under the leadership of Theabone Wolfe Tone declared its end to be "the rights of man in Ireland" and it was to communicate "with similar societies abroad—as the Jacobin Club in Paris, Revolutionary Society in England, the Committee for Reform in Scotland. . . ." With the additional inspiration of the French Revolution, the society spread rapidly to include some half million persons "without reckoning women and old men." [37]

The climax of this rapidly spreading movement was the revolution of 1798. To crush it the government mobilized over 137,000 men and wiped out 50,000 revolutionists. The revolution was abandoned and betrayed by its middle-class supporters. "The capitalists," says Connolly, "sold out, and the lawyers bluffed."

The workers alone carried on the fight. Robert Emmet began secretly to reorganize the rank and file of the society, and it spread again among the workers and peasants throughout the country. A day was set for a new revolt, but the movement was betrayed and Sergeant Beatty, its leader, was captured and hanged in Dublin.

The rebellion was quelled, but the hatred of the Irish masses, the deep hatred of an oppressed class for its oppressors, was not. Children learned it from their mothers; as they grew up it was imbedded deeply in their thought, and expressed itself in speech, song and action. Thousands of Irish workers and peasants drank to the toast:

> Here is that every Irishman
>   May stand to the cause,
> And subdue the British government
>   And its coercion laws.

In the five years between 1845 and 1850 there was famine in Ireland. Hundreds of thousands perished of hunger and the disease that added additional horror to the lives of the Irish poor.

Foreign oppression, bitter exploitation, the theft of land and unbearable poverty, life always in the shadow of the British hangman's noose, drove thousands of Irish workers to foreign lands. A great many of them, baptized in the fire of the class struggle in Ireland, emigrated to America. Many came into the coal regions of Pennsylvania, where they found class war in a new guise, but class war nonetheless. Here, as in Ireland, were starvation, exploitation, the lack of the right to organize—and national hatred. Over the doors of many employment offices there hung a sign bearing these words:

NO IRISH NEED APPLY

The Irish miners turned again to the Ancient Order of Hibernians in their struggle against their exploiters in the new country. The operators and their spokesmen recognized clearly that the pressure for what Dewees calls "unreasonable demands" came from the militant Irish miners around whom they carefully cultivated a legend of crime. They attached to them the epithet "Molly Maguires" and pictured a "secret conspiracy" deliberately planning a campaign of terror and crime. When the miners resorted to force in the heat of strike conflicts, the operators played it up as further evidence of the work of the "Mollies' secret criminal ring." In his book Dewees writes:

The magnitude and length of the "strikes" in the coal region, combined with the influence of those "strikes," not only on business but also on domestic interests throughout a very large section of the country, have drawn special attention to the "Laborers and Miners Union," and an impression has to some extent obtained that the "Labor Union," if not identical, is at least in earnest sympathy with the "Molly Maguires." The only color for such charge exists in the fact that the great majority of the "Mollies" belong to the "Union," and that the counsels of such members were naturally for violent rather than peaceable redress, and, further, that most of the notorious outrages committed by "Mollies" were against capital, as represented in property or in the person of superintendents or bosses. It is also true that decrees of the "Union" were enforced under the influence of a fear of violence against the disobedient, whether members of the "Union" or not—a fear strengthened by the marching of bodies of men from colliery to colliery, demanding an immediate stoppage of work, and the necessity that has arisen to call at different times upon the executive of the State for the military to preserve the peace and protect property. Nevertheless, the charge of sympathy or willing coöperation of the "Labor Union," as a body, with the "Mollies," is believed to be without foundation.[38]

And again Dewees complains:

The control and management of the mines, the manner of their working, the right to employ and discharge hands, were passing away from the owners, and were fast vesting in, not the "Labor Union" proper, but the "Labor Union" under the direction of the Molly Maguires.[39]

The power of the A. O. H. was, of course, much exaggerated by the coal operators in order to frighten capitalist society as a whole and obtain wide support in their fight against the union. Nevertheless, the Irish miners were at the head of the revolt of the working masses in the coal regions of Pennsylvania.

The A. O. H. took an active part in politics. A. K. McClure in his *Old Time Notes of Pennsylvania* says: "The political power of this organization became next to absolute in Schuylkill County, and that domination lasted for a number of years." [40] It lasted in fact until the operators had secured the legal murder of the most active members and crushed the organization in the anthracite district. Dewees also complained that the Irish miners "sought not only to control the movements of the 'Labor Union,' to inspire whole mining interests with a fear of their displeasure, but also to have a potent voice in the politics, township, county, state, and national." [41]

To fight for control of working conditions through a union, and, in addition, to seek influence in the government, even though it be capitalist government and therefore completely ineffective as an instrument to protect or advance the interests of labor, was, of course, a crime on the part of the workers.

Later, in the farcical trial of Thomas Munley, the spokesman and leader of the coal operators, Franklin B. Gowen, president of the Philadelphia and Reading Coal and Iron

Company, acting as prosecutor, couched in the following vindictive terms the complaint of the mine owners against the A. O. H.:

Criminal in its character, criminal in its purpose, it had frequently a political object. You will find the leaders of this society the prominent men in the townships. Through the instrumentality of their order and its power, they were able to secure offices for themselves. You see here, and now know, that one of the commissioners of this county is a member of this order. . . .[42]

A struggle which brought forth such hatred and brutal oppression from the operators must have been, of necessity, a bitter one. The short-lived and vacillating struggles of the past, which had been almost totally ineffectual in obtaining any improvement in the miners' conditions, culminated in the Long Strike of 1875.

CHAPTER IV

THE LONG STRIKE OF 1875

WITH the strike of 1875 the decisive struggle, long smoldering between the coal interests and the miners, sometimes flaming briefly, broke into a great fire. It was the first important open contest of forces in the coal region. Its defeat gave the operators an upper hand and opened the way for the destruction of the existing miners' organizations. It forced the coal miners' fight underground into the Ancient Order of Hibernians—the "Molly Maguires." That the strike was of the first importance was well recognized by the operators, who saw in its defeat a path to the return of the pre-union days when the most abominable conditions must be accepted without protest; and the fight to break the unions was carried through in the most unscrupulous, determined and uncompromising manner.

Preparations were made with care and precision. The mine owners mobilized all their resources for the struggle. They went into the fight, not blindly, but according to a well organized plan of campaign.

Throughout the seventies the great coal companies had united all their forces and their wealth to wipe out the rising trade union movement.* The growing power of the miners

* In the anonymous, *The Lives and Times of the Molly Maguires,* published in 1877, we find the following:

"Owing to the tyranny exercised by the Mollies and by their leaders, through the Miners' Union in 1871 and 1872, the prosperity of the coal regions and the value of property in Schuylkill and adjoining counties was a source of real fear to the operators. "The great companies," wrote Dewees, "combined in a struggle for the ownership of their property, and in the struggle have been materially assisted by the prostration of business under which we at present suffer." [43]

At the head of the mine owners' combination was the Philadelphia and Reading Railroad and its subsidiary, the Philadelphia and Reading Coal and Iron Company with Franklin B. Gowen, its president, as leader. But all other major coal interests joined with him and the Reading, and Dewees could write of "Charles W. Parrish, Esq., the president of the Lehigh and Wilkes-Barre Coal Company," that "to render the land of his company valuable, he, like Mr. Gowen, was fully impressed with the necessity of lessening the overgrown power of the 'Labor Union' and of absolutely exterminating, if possible, the Molly Maguires." [44]

The government, the press, the church, the power of millions of dollars, were at the service of the operators. They had already formed the Coal and Iron Police, that private army, clothed with the police power of the state, which has long been infamous in labor history as the Pennsylvania Cossacks. The operators demanded a free hand in the industry. They would tolerate no degree of control by the miners over the conditions of their life and work.

From the miners' side the strike was a spontaneous uprising. The leadership of the Workingmen's Benevolent Association was fearful of open conflict and rather willing to stand a loss of power and worsened working conditions than to stand battle for improvements. They resisted the

began to be seriously affected. It was seen that unless decisive and effective measures should be adopted the Mollies would in time gain supreme control of affairs, values would depreciate, and honest men would be forced to leave the coal regions or join the bloodthirsty and mercenary organization." (pp. 61-62.)

pressure of the rank and file who were readier for a chance to test their strength. And when the pressure had become too great to resist and the strike was a fact, they openly denounced the militant policy which gave the only hope for victory, demanding "peaceful behavior" and legality, no matter what the law demanded.

A proper reverence for the organization and its forms was of greater moment to the officialdom than decisive action; questions of constitution were above the strike, above wage cuts, far above the sufferings of the men, women and children in the coal patches. On April 21, 1875, in the very midst of battle, President John Siney of the Miners' National Association called a meeting of its Executive Board to ask this querulous and somewhat breathless question:

Is the constitution [of the union] to be sovereign and imperative in the control of the members, or is it to be used merely as a shield under which to organize, and then its more vitals parts renounced by single lodges, districts, or states when the Executive assumes to enforce obedience to its dictates whenever those may deem it prudent on their account so to do, and yet claim allegiance to this institution?

And while the greatest strike in anthracite history was being waged all about him, Siney saw nothing incongruous in making this statement to his Executive Board:

The matter of "strikes," I need scarcely say, is the source of most of our (sic) troubles, and in their origin and control is where we find insubordination and disregard to the constitutional law predominant with our members. The intelligent use of this instrument, as a means of defense, is one of the prime objects of this association. That the indiscriminate and "blind-man-buff" system of striking and conducting them was, has been, and is, the cause of degrading our own class, our first convention recognized, and the last convention affirmed, and every day affords us new and powerful proofs. On this recognition the strike-laws in our constitution were framed so as to institute courts of conciliation and arbitration, as a substitute by which to settle the disputes of our trade that must inevitably arise between employer and employed—wherever cases arose that could be so settled. Some cases do arise that are extremely difficult to determine whether they can be settled by such a process, but these are rare to be found.[45]

And in May, 1875, the *Miners' National Record* stated that: "We are bitter opponents of strikes, and can see a justification of them as a last resort only against pure and unadulterated oppression or injustice on the part of the employers of labor."

Such sentiments, implying that the strikes were the result of wanton irresponsibility on the part of the miners, altogether neglecting the danger, poverty, degradation and misery of their lives in the pits, were attacks against thei. cause. This same opportunist policy was carried on by the officials of the United Mine Workers of America who, from the very beginning of the organization, declared their official goal to be conferences and arbitration rather than strikes. The officials of the Miners' National Association played into the hands of the operators during the Long Strike, as John Mitchell, John Lewis and William Green (later to become president of the American Federation of Labor) of the U. M. W. A. did more adroitly and more completely in the struggle of later years.[46]

The great strike of 1875 was a real war in which the armies of two classes faced each other. On one side were the operators, organized into the Anthracite Board of Trade, generaled by the Philadelphia and Reading Iron and Coal Company, commanding vast resources of wealth and the power of the state. Against them were the miners, poor, hampered by the officials of their organization, but with a wonderful spirit of sacrifice, an unswerving militancy, and a powerful determination to win.

They vowed never to return to the pits for reduced wages. They marched, singing. Many songs sprang out of the strike, which record its every aspect. Of scabs, "blacklegs":

> They are a disgrace to their race, wherever they may be—
> Traitors to their fellow miners, likewise to society.

And:

> Now two long months are nearly over—that no one can deny,
> And for to stand another we are willing for to try,
> Our wages shall not be reduced, tho' poverty do reign.
> We'll have seventy-four basis, boys, before we work again.

Although the miners' resistance struck the operators a blow which they certainly felt, it did not induce them to yield a single point. They were determined to win; their victory meant the destruction of the union.

In Clearfield County, central Pennsylvania, in the meanwhile, the bituminous miners had struck for a rate increase of 10 cents a ton. After the strike had lasted for three weeks strike-breakers were imported and the authorities were called on to protect them. John Siney, president of the Miners' National Association, and Xingo Parks, its field organizer, were arrested and charged with conspiracy when they attempted to speak to the Clearfield County strikers. A few days later, on May 13, twenty-six miners were arrested at Houtzdale on the same charge. Siney was acquitted; Parks and the twenty-six men of the rank and file were convicted of conspiracy and riot and each sentenced to a year in jail.

As the Long Strike continued and the threat of starvation

hung heavier over the strikers' shacks, the union yielded on the wage question. But the miners still demanded that even if rates were to be lowered the union must have a voice in the settlement of rates. The coal companies, however, refused to admit them into any negotiations whatsoever. Thus, the power of the miners to control the conditions of their work and life was, more even than immediate demands, the center of the strike. It was so recognized by both sides, and as the operators sensed weakness in their opponents, they became more aggressive.

The rôle of the courts in this bitter struggle between labor and capital is aptly indicated by the judge's charge to the jury in the Siney-Parks case.

"Any agreement, combination or confederation to increase the price of any vendable commodity, whether labor, merchandise or anything else," the court declared, "is conspiracy." [47]

And in the Joyce-Maloney case, also arising out of this strike, the judge used these words in pronouncing sentence: "I find you, Joyce, to be president of the union, and you, Maloney, to be secretary, and therefore I sentence you to one year's imprisonment." [48]

The effect of such pronouncements on the miners and on their methods of struggle must be plain. Trade unionism became by definition a crime, conspiracy; union activity itself—no legalistic subterfuge was needed—was punishable by imprisonment.

"I find you, Joyce, to be president of the union, . . . and *therefore* I sentence you. . . ."

Where, now, was the legality that "level-headed leaders" had advocated? The coal miners were rapidly being forced to the point where they must give up activity altogether and go back to the tender mercies of the companies who refused to overcome "a large amount of explosive gas generated in this mine," and at the best made "but fair promises, which were never intended to be fulfilled"; or there must be a change of tactics, recourse to an underground organization with which to wage a further war.

The government's attack had weakened the union forces in the anthracite region. The Executive Board of the Miners' National Association appealed to "the officers, members and other friends" for aid. "Men of Pennsylvania," the appeal read, "their fate to-day is your fate to-morrow. If these men are criminally guilty, so are you—so is every trade unionist in the land and they are few from the flock who are chosen as an expiation for the sins of the whole." [49]

The sympathies of workers throughout the country were with the miners. The Industrial Congress of the United States,* meeting in Indianapolis on April 13, a month before the conspiracy arrests, unanimously adopted a resolution in support of the anthracite miners, tendering "heart-felt sympathies to the miners now locked out, and earnestly requesting all organized bodies of working men throughout the country to forward to the Treasurer of this Congress as

* The Industrial Congress was organized July 15, 1873, in Cleveland, Ohio, at the convention of the conservative trade unions which were opposed to independent political action on the part of the workers and withdrew from the National Labor Union, bringing about its disintegration. It was another attempt to federate the "pure and simple" trade unions on a national scale very much in the same form as the present American Federation of Labor. The policies of the Industrial Congress and its affiliated trade unions were those of class collaboration and arbitration as opposed to strikes. At the second convention held in Rochester, N. Y., April 14, 1874, the Industrial Congress was merged with the Industrial Brotherhood and the latter's name was adopted. Its third and last convention took place at Indianapolis, April 13, 1875, with only twenty-three delegates present. The national trade unions failed to send their representatives. The convention decided to set July 4, 1876, as the date for the establishment of the eight-hour day, but the Industrial Brotherhood itself disintegrated.

generous financial assistance as their circumstances will permit."

On the basis of this resolution, Jack H. Wright, president of the Congress, issued a further appeal to the workers of the country:

These men, with all their sufferings and wrongs, are now engaged in a contest with the most powerful Anti-Trade Union combination that has ever been formed in this country. . . . This combination now demands a reduction in the prices of labor, of from 30 to 40 per cent, when a reduction of 20 per cent has been already effected.

He noted that most of the capital in the anthracite combination was British, and continued:

Those who are controlling it are robbing both miners and consumers for the benefit of the Shylocks of London and Liverpool. They [the miners] have been denounced as conspirators, vilified by the press, and charged with lawlessness and crime. . . . The military power of the State has and is being used to annoy them into submission. . . . These miners are fighting the battles of labor in this country, . . . their defeat heralds your assault. . . . Your duty demands that you sustain them.[50]

The Workingmen's Advocate, a Chicago publication, warned the employers against pressing the workers too far:

Now we assure the pirates and scoundrels who are pursuing such a suicidal course, that they are playing with edged tools. . . . The threat of crushing John Siney will only recoil on their own heads. Today, a mirror reflects a single lion; let them break it, and a thousand will confront them. . . . Behind Mr. Siney stand the workingmen of the United States, and if the coal corporations of Pennsylvania think they can successfully defy them, let them force the issue.[51]

In the sixth month of the strike the miners were destitute. They were ill-clothed, badly housed, and starving. Still they had no idea of surrender, they would rather intensify the strike and still struggle for victory. On June 3, about a thousand men assembled to march from colliery to colliery to call out those men who were still at work. Dewees' description of the march is worth quoting if for nothing else than the light it throws on the operators' attitude:

During the night and early in the morning of the 3rd, the mob began to gather at Glover's hill, . . . just opposite the West Shenandoah Colliery, then in operation, and it was upon this colliery that it was intended the first demonstration should be made to compel the men to quit work. Preparations for protection were, however, made. Captain Linden, with a force of twenty-four of the Coal and Iron Police armed with Winchester rifles, was on hand early in the morning. About six o'clock some five hundred of the mob which had assembled on Glover's Hill moved over to the colliery, where they were met by Captain Linden, his force drawn up in line of battle. No engagement took place; the firm stand of a few determined men kept the whole crowd at bay; but for about six hours the mob was turbulent and threatening.

About twelve o'clock the rioters retreated and joined the party on Glover's Hill. A line was then formed, and, preceded by a drum corps, they marched to Mahonoy City, some five miles distant, gathering force as they went along. At Mahonoy City they met the sheriff of Schuylkill County and his posse. The sheriff attempted to protect the working collieries. The excitement increased. Shots were fired on both sides, and several of the rioters were injured. The sheriff was, however, compelled to retreat, leaving Mahonoy City in possession of the rioters. The lock-up was broken open, and all work in that locality stopped for the day. The line was then again formed, and the mob left Mahonoy with the avowed intention of stopping the work at West Shenandoah. Loud threats of vengeance on the workmen [that is, the strike-breakers] at the colliery and at the Coal and Iron Police were heard, but either fear of Captain Linden and his gallant little band, or better counsels, prevailed, and before they reached that point the mob was dispersing.[52]

The power of the operators, the bitter opposition of the courts and other organs of the state—and hunger—finally had their way. The miners were beaten. "The organization was broken. The heart was knocked out of the brave fellows who built up and sustained it," said Joseph F. Patterson, one of the strike leaders and the last secretary of the Workingmen's Benevolent Association. "Its power was gone. It was shortly to become but a memory." [53]

There was still sentiment for a continuation of the struggle, but it was given up. For this officials were accused of having sold out to the operators, and the miners' bitterness at their deflection has been carried down to us in a song of the period:

> What if this union was forsaken forever,
>   And poor men made slaves as they've been before,
> To make matters worse, they must work for small wages;
>   They can ne'er pay their bills that they own in the store.
>
> If they had been united and pulled all together,
>   And kept politics within their own bounds—
> But when they were elected, the poor man was neglected;
>   They sold the men's freedom to Franklin B. Gowen.

The miners were aware that their defeat did not end the class struggle. Their militant spirit was not crushed and they hoped to rise again some day against their enemies. In the same song they said:

> When the men go back to work, they must all be determined
> To prepare for a struggle in some future day.

Their hope was not in vain. The anthracite miners many times rose and fought heroically against the coal barons during the following fifty years. The strike of 1875 paved the way for the stubborn battles to come in which the miners would direct the struggle against their own misleaders as well as against the coal barons.

While the rank and file miners, after the defeat of the strike of 1875, returned to work with the determination "to prepare for a struggle in some future day," their leaders surrendered to the employers completely. "Labor and capital will go hand in hand and be no more known as arrayed against each other," they declared through the *Miners' National Record* of August, 1875. "Their interests will be truly identical and recognized as such. The workman will get the true value of his labor, and invested capital will get its own." This brotherhood between labor and capital was to be achieved through a coöperative movement. As far as the leaders were concerned there were to be no more strikes, nor class struggles of any kind.

It was now suggested that the Miners' National Association itself go into the mining business. "Coöperative production," said the *Miners' National Record,* "we have been accustomed, with many other labor reforms, to look forward to as the only true solution of the labor problem. When the owner of the capital engaged in any branch of industry is also the owner of labor, that is, in partnership with it, then we will have peace and harmony in the process of production. Strikes with their causes will have vanished and we no longer will have occasion to complain of the tyranny of aggregated capital on the one hand, or the owners of capital to cry out against the unjust accusations of the trade unions on the other."

The union officials decided to purchase a tract of land in Tennessee and to open mines for the union. Siney made a trip to the territory and purchased the land, but in the next year the organization completely disintegrated without having opened a single mine.

Those who had led the strike were blacklisted and subjected to consistent persecution. Few, if any, of them could find employment in the county where they had lived and worked all of their lives. Some left the state altogether, hopeful of finding employment elsewhere. But the blacklist followed them. When mine superintendents found out who they were and from where they had come, they were forced to move on once more. Active unionists who were reëmployed became the prey of every superintendent and petty boss, who visited upon them humiliation and ridicule and assigned them to the worst and least profitable working places.[54]

After the strike was broken, wages were cut again and again. Patterson tells us that in 1876, 1877, 1878, and 1879, the miners "received 48, 58, 50 and 51 cents respectively less than in 1869 for doing the same dollar's worth of work."

"Well, we've been beaten, beaten all to smash," was a line in a song, popular among the miners of the time, which continued:

> And, now, sir, we've begun to feel the lash,
> As wielded by a gigantic corporation,
> Which runs the commonwealth and ruins the nation.

And again:

> And thus the matter stands. We do not dare
> To look a boss in the face and whisper "Bah,"
> Unless we wish to join the mighty train
> Of miners wandering o'er the earth like Cain,
> And, should you wish to start upon a tramp
> O'er hillock, mountain, valley, plain and swamp,

Or travel as the Pilgrim of John Bunyan,
One talismanic word will do it, "Union,"
Just murmur that, and all the laws of the State
Or congress will not save you from your fate;
They'll drive you out, forfeit your goods, degrade you,
Just as the British did in old Acadia.

And in another song:

Our wages, John, grow beautifully less,
And if they keep on growing thus, I guess,
We'll have to put on magnifying specs,
To see the little figures on our checks.
It's nothing strange to find on seeing the docket
We've worked a month and still are out of pocket.
It makes a man feel dirty cheap, you bet,
To work a month and then come out in debt.

The operators exulted. The strike was lost; the union
was smashed and the miners, singing their troubles, lifted
their voices to warn other workers from the district:

If in exchange for the labor of a day
You wish to have an honest, fair day's pay;
If you do wish to have just rights among
Those of freedom, action, speech and tongue;
If you do wish to have a fair supply
Of wholesome food, be buried when you die
With decent rites—by this I mean at least
Sufficient to distinguish man from beast,
Stay where you are, or if you must go hence,
Go East, or North, or South, no consequence.
Take any one direction you'll be blest
Sooner with what you seek than coming West.
In short, if you wish to enjoy God's bounty,
Go anywhere except to Schuylkill County.[55]

CHAPTER V

THE LIFE AND DEATH STRUGGLE IN PENNSYLVANIA

DESPITE the defeat of the Long Strike of 1875 and the destruction of the Union, the militant Irish miners continued their struggle against bitter exploitation, tyranny and terror. When the mine owners resorted to outright murder as a method of subduing them, the miners turned to the Ancient Order of Hibernians, the only organization left them, and utilized it as an organized center for self-defense and for carrying on their struggle against the employers. The A. O. H., which in other sections of the country was bourgeois, nationalistic and respectable, became, in the hands of the miners, a weapon to be used in the class struggle.

The warfare became guerrilla in character. There were no more great open battles such as the strike of 1875 had been. It was a struggle which necessarily had to assume a new form. Every miner had to become a guerrilla warrior, defending himself the best he could against the organized power of the mine owners, their provocateurs and their government. The A. O. H. in the anthracite served as the secret organizational center of the miners through which they combated the intensified starvation and misery which the employers imposed upon them after the unsuccessful strike, and which they used as a basis in their effort to reëstablish their union.

The end of the strike saw all the more reason for the

miners to organize. The operators took advantage of the miners' defeat by imposing even worse conditions upon them. The *Labor Standard,* of August 26, 1876, declares that "the reports during the past week from the Pennsylvania coal regions are truly distressing. Many families have been reported as having been subsisting on the flesh of domestic animals which they were compelled to eat to prevent starvation. Numerous instances of *actual starvation* have been recorded in Wyoming and Lackawanna counties." The militant miners continued to organize their struggle against starvation.

The operators now sought the complete annihilation of all the forces that opposed them. They were intent upon wiping out every trace of resistance among the miners to the semi-feudal conditions in the coal fields. They directed their campaign against the new organized center of the miners, the A. O. H. The charges of murder which they so carefully prepared against the organizers and the most militant miners would send them to the gallows and become a means by which all forms of labor organization was to be destroyed. This was repeatedly and frankly admitted by Franklin B. Gowen, who was not only the leader of the operators in their anti-union, anti-labor activities, but in some of the miners' trials prosecuted them as chief counsel for the Commonwealth.

In the trial of John Kehoe, who was one of the miners executed, he said:

The gentlemen tell us that this society [the Ancient Order of Hibernians] is a good society; but we try it [!] by its acts. We try it, not by its written declaration, or by its printed books, but according to the evidence in this case, and by that alone your verdict which, as I said before, will not only convict the prisoners of the offense with which they are charged, but in the estimation of the people of this county, and of the whole country, *will convict this society* [author's italics] so that it will never hereafter lift its head to look man in the face, and above all, that not a member will hereafter lift his hand to strike the blow that has so often carried terror to the community, which now looks to us as its last refuge.[56]

Dewees, also very frank on this question, said that Gowen "has been engaged in a bitter contest, and the immense power of the coal combination in connection with the depressed condition of business [the panic of 1873] has given him the victory. *He has taken full advantage of his position as victor in waging war, not upon the laboring man, but upon the 'Labor Union.'*" (Author's italics.) [57]

In the issue dated June 1, 1876, a correspondent of the *Irish World*, writing from the anthracite district, declared that the mine owners, by means of propaganda creating a general belief in a "reign of terror," wanted "to make Molly Maguirism such a frightful bugaboo that no workingman will henceforth dare to protest against any act of the boss, however arbitrary and unusual, lest the awful charge should be hurled at him: 'You are a Molly!'" And it is plain now that many criminal acts, committed by Pinkerton labor spies, were charged to the "Molly Maguires."

But what had really happened in the anthracite area after the Long Strike? What was the "blow that has so often carried terror to the community" that no miner would, hereafter dare "lift his hand to strike"?

Before and during the strike and in the years immediately following, the coal operators organized armed bands and vigilance committees whose aim was to terrorize the miners into submission. They murdered mine workers with impunity, and used their guns without fear of punishment. "Many operators," wrote Dr. Roberts, "then furnished arms to their foremen, and only wanted men who could use them. . . . When labor in many instances sought relief, it was answered with an oath supplemented with the pointing of a revolver." [58]   In the Wiggan's Patch murder of 1875, these terrorists had attacked the home of a family named O'Donnell and shot and killed Charles O'Donnell and Mrs. Charles McAllister.   Other members of the family succeeded in escaping.*   Other killings were common; and in each case the blow was struck at some one active in the workers' organization.

At Tuscarora, a hundred miners met and demanded a redress of their grievances.   The mine boss and vigilantes came out and began shooting into the crowd.   A few miners were wounded and one killed.   The killer was arrested and brought to trial, but found not guilty on the pretext that he had "protected himself from the mob of assassins."

On another occasion, a mine boss named Patrick Varry opened fire into a crowd of about three hundred men.   With considerable and apparent satisfaction Gowen tells us how well the bullets were aimed, and how, as the miners "fled [they] left long tracks of their blood behind them."   Varry

---

* Dewees gives the following description of this bloody affair:
Friday and Charles O'Donnell resided, in December, 1875, with their mother at Wiggan's Patch, a small colliery town near Mahonoy City. Charles McAllister, with his wife, who was a daughter of Mrs. O'Donnell, also boarded in the same house.   About one o'clock on the morning of the 1st of December, an attack by a mob of disguised men roused the sleeping family.   Friday O'Donnell . . . sought safety in instant flight from the house . . . Charles McAllister also succeeded in escaping. James McAllister was captured, had a rope placed around his neck, but succeeded in getting away, though in doing so he received a severe gun shot wound in the arm.   Charles O'Donnell was captured, and was dragged a short distance from the house, where he was shot and instantly killed; fourteen bullets are said to have been lodged in his body.   Whilst this was occurring, Mrs. Charles McAllister made her appearance in her night clothes at the door of the house.   Shots were fired at her, which, taking effect, caused almost instant death. . . . A paper containing the words, "The Murderers of Uren and Sanger" was next morning found near the scene of the outrage.—*The Molly Maguires*, pp. 237-238.

was never arrested or in any way prosecuted for this murderous assault.

Allan Pinkerton (of whose activities more later) admits that, more than once, members of the Ancient Order of Hibernians were quietly murdered. Thus, in March, 1875, one Edward Coyle, a leading member of the Hibernians, was found dead in the slip of Plank Colliery, property of the Philadelphia and Reading Coal and Iron Company. And in the same month, a certain Bradley, a mine engineer, shot and killed an active member of the Ancient Order of Hibernians at Mine Hill Gap.[59]

There is no doubt that force was answered with force, and that the miners fought terror with whatever means there were at hand. The violence of the operators and their agents reached the point at which even the conservative Miners' National Association appealed to its members to arm themselves and protect their lives and homes. On October 27, 1874, at the second convention of the M. N. A., held at Cleveland, the following resolution was introduced:

Whereas, The operators of the country in a number of instances have seen fit to supplant their workingmen for the crime of having asked for their own, with armed banditti and lazzaroni from the slums of the large cities; and

Whereas, The governments, both state and national, in having permitted the said banditti and lazzaroni to carry deadly firearms in a time of profound peace, practically admitted the right of every American citizen to the same; therefore

Resolved, That we recommend the members of the several miners' associations throughout the country to immediately provide themselves with a full supply of the best breech-loading rifles which the country affords.[60]

Commenting on an editorial in the New York *Sun*—written in the usual venomous style—the *Labor Standard* (August 26, 1876) declared:

It may certainly be a cause for regret that men should combine in secret organizations but it is more to be regretted that men should be compelled to join them as the only means left for the protection of their existence. It is no secret that in many parts of the country workmen dare not publicly belong to a trade union and are consequently forced to meet in secret. Men like the "Molly Maguires," as they are called, who are starved and outraged cannot be expected to be over particular in their means of redress, and considering the terrible provocation they receive, should not be adjudged guilty.

It was open class warfare. The militant Irish miners put up a determined struggle. Their strike methods, embodying the use of mass picketing and armed defense against police and the company thugs are those traditional to revolutionary workers throughout the world. They have been employed by American labor since, in numerous struggles, and have been just as viciously opposed by the employers, as in the struggle of the textile workers of Gastonia, N. C., in 1929, when seven strike leaders and mill workers were sentenced to long prison terms for defending themselves and the tent colony of the strikers from an armed onslaught of police and company thugs.

In the bitter warfare in the anthracite there were casualties on both sides, although more on the miners' than on the operators' side. But the mine bosses and superintendents, killed in the class war as the result of a reign of terror instituted by the operators themselves, served as the pretext for Gowen and his associates, and for the government, to attack and exterminate the militant leadership of the miners and thereby to crush their organized power.

The miners' organizations—the Workingmen's Benevolent Association and the Ancient Order of Hibernians in the anthracite fields—were dangerous to the coal barons,

who were determined to exterminate them and with them
the resistance of the workers in the pits.

We have already mentioned the connection between the
struggle in Ireland and England and that in the Pennsylvania anthracite counties. How close this connection was,
and how important in the present struggle, is suggested by
the *Irish World* for August 5, 1876, where, in an article by
T. A. Devyr, we find this statement:

Take, for example, the Philadelphia and Reading Coal and Iron
Company. They project a monopoly so immense that they are
forced to fraternize, or conspire, with the millionaires of London
to enable them to carry it out. These millionaires furnish $20,000,-
000 as their share of the pool, and, armed with this resource, their
agent [Gowen] returns to Pennsylvania, buys up and gets a bad
title to the coal fields, and sets to work the white slaves that live
by wages in that region.

That the Pennsylvania war was followed closely in
Britain is revealed in an article that appeared as late as
twenty years after the Long Strike of 1875 and whose author
still had only praise for the extermination of the miners'
organization.

The notion of any one pausing for a moment to consider the
ways and means by which these human tigers [the miners] were
destroyed would be inconceivable to any but a Hibernian mind.
When an Irishman, caught red-handed from murder, was placed in
danger of his life, a howl of anguish and indignation from every
Irish community in the country rent the air.[61]

Yet this same author might have discovered that many
of the Pennsylvania miners were not Irish, but Welsh,
Scotch and English who had, in the collieries of their own
country, a history of exploitation so bitter that Andrew
Roy, an Ohio mine inspector and a student of mining his-

tory, could write, as late as 1876, that the British miners were "in a low and dependent state, and the earlier acts of mining legislation were passed . . . for the purpose of enslaving them." [62]   And Alexander Trachtenberg notes that "actual slavery existed in the Scottish mines till the end of the eighteenth century, the miners being transferred with the mines."   Here, too, are quoted horrible details of mine life taken down from the lips of eleven-year-old Janet Cumming, a little Scotch mine girl who, in 1842, carried "the large bits of coal from the wall face to the pit bottom and the small pieces, called the chows, to a creel.   The weight is usually a hundred-weight.   Do not know how many pounds, but it is some weight to carry." [63]

The miners, on their side, had brought with them out of their experiences in struggle in Ireland and England a full understanding of the principle of organization.   They knew that they were a power to be feared by the operators only as long as they were organized effectively and their experience in underground organizations fighting for Irish freedom had given them knowledge of how to organize secretly and build their strength until they were ready to come out into the open and give battle.

Their struggles back home had also reached a higher political level.   The English miners had learned how to combine the struggle in the legislatures with the open class conflict to their advantage, although the early efforts at reform had failed, bitterly fought by the mine owners because these bills were "mistaken humanity" and committed the "injustice of interfering between the laborer and the manner in which he might choose to employ himself." [64] Lord Londonderry, who, as leader of the Tories, controlled Parliament, was also a big mine owner, just as Gowen, president of the biggest coal combination in the anthracite, controlled the legislature and acted as state prosecutor

Gowen took his lessons in class war from his English associates. How close his connection was with the British capitalists and how keen the interest of these latter was in the destruction of the Pennsylvania miners' organizations may be deduced from the fact that about the time the mine leaders were hanged in June, 1877, Gowen hastened to London to report to the stockholders of his company there.

In its issue of July 6 of the same year, the *Daily Miners' Journal* carried an editorial, commenting on this trip and its "fortunate" result. It concluded:

Mr. Gowen must feel both gratified and strengthened by this unqualified [British] endorsement of his plans. His future is now brighter than at any time in the past year, and it is scarcely possible that there are still unforseen misfortunes awaiting him which will prevent his triumphant success in the end.

As it had in Ireland, the Catholic Church took an active part in Pennsylvania, on the side of the operators, as might be expected. Gowen himself declared that Archbishop Wood of Philadelphia was the only person to whom he confided the plans for importing detectives and provocateurs, and otherwise working to smash the miners' organizations, as long as six or seven years before they fructified.

And in the proper course of time the Archbishop publicly denounced and excommunicated all members of the Ancient Orders of Hibernians in the anthracite area.

In 1874, Dewees says, a group of Catholic priests issued a denunciation of the Hibernians, which included the following points:

1. Ribbonmen and kindred societies have been *nominati* condemned by the Holy See.

2. A society in America organized on the same basis, holding the same principles, and animated by the same spirit, comes within the condemnation of its prototype in Ireland.

4. The testimony of members, ex-members, public report and our experience compel us to believe that the A. O. H. has all the vices of societies *nominatim* condemned in Ireland.

5. Experience has proved that no faith is to be placed in the most solemn promises or denials of the A. O. H. . . . .

8. Evidence sufficient to convince the most skeptical has come to light that works forbidden by the commandment "thou shalt not kill" are traceable to the A. O. H.

9. The spirit and acts of the A. O. H. are clearly condemned by the plainest teachings of the Decalogue.

Rev. D. J. McDermott, in a published letter dated May 11, 1876, declared that the A. O. H. was a "diabolical secret society, and that it is everywhere the same society in spirit and government." [65]

The operators used the backing of the Catholic Church to its fullest advantage as a means of rousing the religious prejudice of the masses against the miners. The Irish coal workers, themselves good Catholics, were confronted with what was to them a terrible threat. They were offered the alternative, either of giving up their organization and their struggle against the coal interests, or of being cursed and excommunicated from the church.

During the trials themselves, Gowen used the Catholic Church very effectively to prejudice the jury against the miners. During the Munley trial, for instance, he turned to the jury and shouted:

Was there ever such sublime, such tremendous impudence in the world, as that a member of this secret society, a society which has been denounced by its own church, and each member of which has been excommunicated by the Archbishop of Philadelphia and by the Pope himself, outcasts from society, and from the Communion of their own religion, the door of the church shut in their faces and the gates of heaven closed against them by the excommunication of their priests—these men, infidels and atheists, caring for no church and worshipping no God, set themselves up in this community as the representatives of the Catholic faith.[66]

To millions of Catholics throughout the country the condemnation by the church was sufficient to prove that the miners' organizations were composed exclusively of cold-blooded criminals, that the accused were unquestionably guilty of the crimes as charged and that no tear should be shed if they were executed *en masse.*

Into the life and death struggle which raged in the Pennsylvania anthracite regions during the seventies of the last century, the coal operators introduced an element entirely new to the class battles of this country. Here for the first time an organized system of labor spies appeared on the scene, although, of course the individual spy had always been an aspect of many previous class battles. F. B. Gowen, spokesman for and leader of the coal interests, was the pioneer in the field. The Pinkerton Detective Agency was engaged by him to supply spies and provocateurs. Gowen made open acknowledgment of his activity in this direction during the Munley trial. "I knew," he declared, "that it could only be done by secret detectives, and I had enough experience, both as a lawyer and as the head of a very large corporation, to know that public municipal detectives . . . are the very last persons to whom you could trust a mission and an enterprise such as this." [67]

From that time the labor spy system has become firmly established in the United States. It has been blessed, then and later, both by the church and state.[68]

We have already pointed out the support that Archbishop Wood gave Gowen in this matter. And when the counsel for the defense in one of the miners' trials objected to the testimony of James McParlan, the chief Pinkerton spy, the judge declared: "We employ spies in wars between nations; is it any worse to employ them in wars in society?"

His Honor, who—mind you—according to the claims of bourgeois democracy was supposed to be sitting in an "impartial" court, had for the moment lost his judicial composure and revealed his own function and that of the assassin and spy McParlan "in wars in society"!

Gowen declared that he had arranged with the Pinkertons for the service of a single spy, one James McParlan, who operated under the name of McKenna. McParlan was an Irishman himself. He was instructed—both Gowen and Pinkerton maintained, though we shall have ample opportunity to discover otherwise—to do no more than use his Irish birth as a means of entering the "secret organization" of the miners, discover "everything about its workings," and report back to Pinkerton who would pass his findings on to Gowen.

As a matter of fact, the plan agreed on between Pinkerton and Gowen in 1871-1872 was much more ambitious than any of this might lead one to believe. The coal operators raised among themselves and paid to the Pinkerton Agency at least $100,000 at the very start. Preparations for an onslaught from this direction were made on an enormous scale. The Pinkerton Agency sent among the miners, not the solitary McParlan, but scores of spies and provocateurs. The coal operators' organ, the *Miners' Weekly Journal*, very franky admitted that a large number of detectives were in the field. The miners, it is said, "do not know how many like him [McParlan] there are among them still. There may be a McParlan in every group of half a dozen that assembles in the back room of somebody's liquor store to plot the murder of a man." [69]

These men were instruments of the operators, sent by them to destroy the miners' organizations—the Workingmen's Benevolent Association and the Ancient Order of Hibernians in the anthracite fields. They were sent to stifle the miners' struggle, even to kill if that proved necessary, and to charge these murders to the leaders of the miners' organizations. And there is no doubt, as we shall see, that they performed their tasks. Recruited from the slums and the ranks of professional criminals, they were ready for anything that might be assigned to them. They are the forerunners of the present-day company thugs and gunmen common to every struggle in the mine fields, from Colorado and Mesaba range to Kentucky and Alabama. D. J. Brown, a former Pinkerton operative who, from the very nature of his activities was well acquainted with the relationship of his employers to the coal operators, wrote in the *Irish World* for June 1, 1876:

McParlan used to be a uniformed watchman and, on account of his dexterity in opening doors and making out imaginary reports, was picked out for the "Molly Maguire" business. Don't you see, these innocent men down there confessed all to him after a ten days' acquaintance. [This refers to the startling ease with which McParlan was able to "extract" the most intimate confessions of the most horrible crimes from men who hardly knew him.] Pinkerton has now received $100,000 from the coal owners and after all this strategy it's a bad point for him that he can't swing a couple Irishmen. He has had men down there running saloons and in every capacity, yet not one has found out anything except McParlan.

Of all the Pinkerton operatives in the anthracite area, the names only of McParlan and a man named Linden were ever revealed, and McParlan alone was called to the witness stand. He was a self-confessed murderer who openly boasted that he had killed a man in Buffalo, New York. Even before any of the Molly Maguire arrests were made, his identity and the nature of his mission had been discovered and his usefulness as a spy, but not as an inventor of crimes, ended.

Yet when he later ascended the witness stand he became a hero. "He was the blood-red wine marked 100," says Gowen. And when his testimony was given, "then we knew we were free men. Then we cared no longer for the Molly Maguires." [70] The *Daily Miners' Journal*, June 29, 1876, added:

> The coal region owes to McParlan a heavy debt of gratitude, for he had saved is not only from the crimes which disgraced it, but from the reign of mob law which would soon have established itself here, to the still greater disgrace of a civilized community.

This savior, it may be noted here, was to reappear on the labor scene some thirty years later when, in 1908, again as a Pinkerton agent, he acted as coach for Harry Orchard in the Moyer-Haywood-Pettibone frame-up. These men, then leaders of the militant Western Federation of Miners, were arrested in Denver, Colorado, kidnaped, and taken to Boise, Idaho, where they were charged with the murder of ex-Governor Stuenenberg. Orchard, a well-known labor spy, admitted the actual killing, but claimed it was done under the influence of the Federation leaders. During Haywood's trial, the Pinkerton connection was brought clearly to the front; workers all over the country rose to demand the release of the kidnaped men, and though President Roosevelt had branded them as "undesirable citizens," the workers' demands were successful. Moyer, Haywood and Pettibone were freed.

McParlan, who had made a spectacular announcement of Orchard's confession and sworn that he would hang the leaders of the Western Federation of Miners, disappeared then.[71]

In the course of the Pennsylvania anthracite struggle it is clear that the Pinkerton agents did not confine themselves to a spy service which often extended to the invention of uncommitted crime, nor even to the activities of the agent provocateur. When they could discover nothing and invention would not serve, they actually committed crime and charged it to the miners. The lawyer who defended John Kehoe correctly noted that murder had increased in the anthracite region during the very years of Pinkerton activity.

It was charged that McParlan "himself assisted to plot, to counsel, to perpetrate" murders [72] and he was, as Gowen himself said, more feared and hated for his ruffianly ways by the men he was supposed to be protecting, than any of those who died on the gallows.

The charges made against this man and the agency which employed him and, so, against the operators whom both represented, are borne out by evidence taken at the trials and by the statements of men in the region not distinguished for their friendship to the miners' cause. Several of those hanged were convicted on the charge of conspiracy to murder on evidence derived almost exclusively from the testimony of McParlan, who claimed with considerable pride *to have known before they were committed, the details of various projected crimes.* McGrath, in his *History of the Ancient Order of Hibernians,* quotes a certain McMahon, who was neither a miner nor a friend of the miners, to this effect:

It must be confessed that many outrages are perpetrated by outside parties and sometimes by minor officials of the company with the view to promote their own interests and with the idea which is always ratified that the suspicion will at once be attached to the Molly Maguires.[73]

CHAPTER VI

THE TRIALS

THE trials, the outcome of which were already determined, served the operators as a platform from which to broadcast over the country the "criminal" character of the miners they were going to execute. With the purpose of still further terrorizing the miners, the operators staged their show at various intervals, using the trials themselves as a means of implicating more miners who were sure to be pounced upon by the "law" and, in their turn, stand trial. It did not make any essential difference upon whom the crimes—real and manufactured—were pinned; the purpose was to "get" the leaders of the miners and as many others as would be sufficient to terrorize and subdue the workers, and force the weaker elements among them to turn state's evidence. The method of frame-up was employed right and left, striking one miner here, another there, although the mine bosses and thugs had been killed in self-defense or in the course of class struggle.

The trials and hangings were staged with all the glamor and sensationalism of a mystery show. They were so much to the delight of the "respectable" elements of the community that on at least one occasion a bevy of young girls, prettily decked out in parasols and ribbons, came in the company of their minister to watch miners' legs dangle in the air while the hangman's rope choked out their life.

Franklin B. Gowen, whom we have seen before as President of the Philadelphia and Reading Coal and Iron Company and leader of the movement to break the miners' unions, acted as state prosecutor in a number of the cases. It was he whom the workers were fighting, he who had hired spies and provocateurs from the Pinkerton organization and initiated the movement to end "the so-called labor unions," and he who had most to gain from the death of the labor leaders. It was he, too, who said, frankly enough: "The name of a Molly Maguire being attached to a man's name is sufficient to hang him." [74]

During the trials, the press of the country, aside from that of workers' organizations and an Irish newspaper or so, came to the aid of the operators by creating an atmosphere of terror around the trials and the men who were being tried. How unscrupulous—and effective—such a newspaper campaign can be will be recognized by any who have seen Sacco and Vanzetti trumpeted as bloody-handed villains; or Tom Mooney handled in columns of type as a despicable murderer; or the Centralia militants, one of whom died, mutilated by the knives and ropes of lynchers, become, in the capitalist press, assassins.

In 1875 and 1876 the miners were represented to the masses of the people as cold-blooded cutthroats, murderers for whom mere death was too easy a punishment.

During the trials the anthracite region was in effect under martial law. The court houses where the trials took place were heavily guarded by the armed forces of the state and by the Coal and Iron Police, placed there to "uphold the majesty of the law" (which might be translated into, "to overawe the miners, to terrorize their witnesses, and to give food for unpleasant thought to any juror who might so far forget himself as to make his decision according to the evidence presented, rather than the desires of the coal barons and their company president-public prosecutor").

Before we go further, however, it may be well to review

one case which preceded the general onslaught, for the light it throws on the methods used then and later. . . .

A year or more before any arrests were made, McParlan was involved in an attempt to "get" one Daniel Dougherty, a young militant miner and a member of the Ancient Order of Hibernians in the anthracite regions. His opportunity came when, on October 31, 1874, George Major, chief burgess of Mahonoy City, was shot and fatally wounded in a fight between two volunteer fire companies, whose pleasant custom it was to make the outbreak of a fire the peg on which to hang an orgy of hooliganism. In this same fight Dougherty was also seriously wounded. He was arrested and charged with Major's murder. The state and the operators put up a number of witnesses who swore that they had actually seen him fire the fatal shot; and the court would neither listen to nor credit the testimony of defense eye-witnesses who were equally positive that a certain John McCann had killed the burgess.

Conviction appeared certain for Dougherty. There was a single hope. He still carried a bullet in his body. The defense contended that the bullet "had been fired from George Major's pistol by William Major and to establish this fact was of great importance, as it would render the innocence of the prisoner manifest." But the operation was dangerous. The defense was desperate. Finally, however, Dougherty decided on the operation and the extracted bullet "fitted George Major's pistol, thus establishing the theory of innocence and Dougherty was triumphantly acquitted." (Dewees, p. 128.) The conspiracy to get Dougherty fell apart.

It is worth noting, however, that neither those who had tried to put him out of the way, nor the witnesses who had perjured themselves, were ever arrested or brought to trial. Later a lawyer defending Kehoe, one of the miners who was executed, drew from McParlan the admission that while Dougherty was on trial, the detective had been aware of his innocence and of the fact that a man named McCann had fired the fatal shot. But McParlan had not testified in the young miner's behalf, and McCann, who had long since left the country, was never brought to trial. McParlan, be it noted, was quite ready to have the innocent Dougherty hanged, not for murder, but for his leadership and militancy among the miners.

So we come to the later trials which spread a two-year terror over anthracite Pennsylvania. We shall not deal, in detail, with all of them, partly because some of the records are no longer to be found, and partly because those still obtainable could fill a book many times larger than the present volume; but chiefly because the cases treated here are typical. What happened in any one or any group sufficiently represents what took place in all of them.

The first trial which was, from the operators' viewpoint, successfully concluded, was that of Michael J. Doyle, a young American-born coal miner. He was one of three men arrested shortly after John P. Jones, a mine superintendent, had been shot and killed.

Doyle, Edward J. Kelly, who like him was young and of American birth, and John Kerrigan, were arrested. The three men had asked for separate trials, which were granted them. But Kerrigan was never tried. He turned state's evidence and helped to send the two other men to death. We shall hear more of him during the course of this story, in his new rôle of labor spy.

With his help and that of McParlan, the prosecution drew into the case another important Hibernian, Alexander Campbell, who was charged with conspiring in the murder of Jones. Campbell had come from Ireland and worked in the mines for a year and a half. Then he opened a hotel, first locating it at Tamaqua, later at Summit Hill. His places were known as headquarters of the Hibernians. He was arrested after the other men. Like Doyle and Kelly he was later convicted and hanged for Jones' death.

Doyle was tried first and his trial was typical of the proceedings against the Irish miners and the officials of their organization. The kind of evidence introduced by the prosecution and accepted by the court clearly revealed prejudice and a hostility which assumed both the guilt of the prisoner and the criminal character of the Ancient Order of Hibernians in the anthracite district. The town was filled with the armed forces of the coal companies and the government, parading through the streets and into the court house corridors; and the court itself was surrounded by Coal and Iron Police. The newspapers kept up a steady barrage of material designed to prejudice the miners' case. *The Pittsburgh Gazette* for May 9, 1876, for instance, declared that:

The Molly Maguires represented the spirit of French Communism and enforced their views by secret murders. The principle involved was simply that of permitting them to dictate the operations of labor. [A horrible thought to employers, who much prefer to dictate terms of labor themselves.] Their men were to be employed, their prices admitted and their directions obeyed. . . .

The absolute extinction of the spirit of lawlessness and murder is essential, . . . and the full disclosure and punishment of the band under consideration is an absolute necessity.

And *The Shenandoah Herald,* for September 17, 1875, during the trials for Jones' murder, said:

It is thought by many that in order to deter the reputable citizens of this place from giving evidence against Kelly, Kerrigan and

Doyle, at present in jail at Mauch Chunk, a citizen or two of the county will be murdered shortly in cold blood. . . . The murderers may be acquitted,—such things have happened before—but the blood of Yost and Jones calls for vengeance, and before the grass of the next spring-time grows upon their graves the debt will have been wiped out, *if not through the agency of the law and the courts, then, and more surely and swiftly, independent of that agency.* (Author's italics.)

During the whole of Doyle's trial, General Albright, as special prosecutor assisting the District Attorney, wore his army uniform. This, of course, impressed on the jury the idea that their patriotic duty required a verdict of guilty. It is important to note that General Albright was the legal adviser of the coal company and that the prosecution was openly "backed with the money, the power, and the influence of the Lehigh and Wilkes-Barre Coal Company." [75]

More than 120 witnesses were brought to court by the prosecution. Seventy came from Lansford, where Jones had been killed, and forty from Tamaqua, a nearby town. The Lansford people testified that they had seen Doyle, Kelly and Kerrigan looking for work in the collieries there. Some had spoken with them or given them food when, hungry and thirsty, they had asked for it. The Tamaqua witnesses testified much to the same effect: They had seen the three men looking for work, had spoken to them or fed them. That was all. And it happened, of course, before the actual killing. It seemed to have little enough bearing on it and it was not contested by the defense. Since the strike there had been a constant flow of miners about the country. Many Hibernians—all whose labor activities were known or suspected—had been blacklisted and driven from their places. They sought work wherever they thought it could be found.

There were two so-called main identification witnesses.

One of them, named Weyhemmer, said that after he heard the shots that killed Jones, he "saw Kelly pull himself along by the bushes up the pipe." But many other state witnesses emphatically denied that there *were any bushes* at the scene of the murder.

Belsner, the other chief witness, said that he actually witnessed the shooting and had noticed a small brass button on the coat of the murderer. But it was later brought out that the shooting had taken place some seventy-five yards from him. When pressed by the defense, Belsner admitted that he had not been able to distinguish the flash of the old-fashioned pistol at that distance. It was something in the nature of the miraculous, then, to have seen a button on a distant coat.

So weak did the case against the miners appear, that the defense did not even put up its own witnesses, contenting itself with the apparently easy refutation of those presented by the prosecution. Later, however, it became clear that it was not necessary, in order to convict a militant miner, to prove the charges against him. The prosecution was working to destroy the Ancient Order of Hibernians in this district. Before the case went to the jurymen they were instructed that Doyle must be convicted, less as the murderer of Jones than as a member of the A. O. H.

When the testimony was concluded, the presiding judge ruled that the Commonwealth should have three speeches to sum up its case, the defense only two. General Albright delivered the principal speech for the prosecution, arguing most violently and demanding the complete extermination of the organization and its every member.

This was utilized by the defense, who charged that the Philadelphia and Reading Coal and Iron Company was seeking the lives of the miners rather than attempting to prove their guilt. Defense attorney Bartholomew said:

For weeks the Coal and Iron Company has been in pursuit of the Molly Maguires, and not of the murderers of John P. Jones. They have given time and money to ferret out the members of that dreaded organization and to crush it because it interferes with their own pecuniary interests. They have caught these men, they imagine them to be Mollies, and in order to crush them and the organization they bring over a hundred witnesses to prove that these men looked for work at their collieries.[76]

General Albright's answer was typical. To a jury principally composed of farmers, he said:

The other side talks of the coal company and calls them little better than a band of murderers, too. What harm did they do to Doyle? If it were not for them everything would go by the board. Where would your farms find a market for their products were it not for the families which the miners of the company support?

And as for the Coal and Iron Police who were gathered in grim military groups within sight of the jurors:

They talk about the Coal and Iron Police and call them hard names. Who are they? They are preservers of peace. This county has no organized police force. What would be done if a rescue of this prisoner were attempted? [Or an acquittal, we might ask.] Would you be responsible for his escape? This court has asked for their aid and they are responsible for the safe-keeping of him until you have set him free or sent him to his God. These men are called to stand between you and a mob and see that no violence is done to you for the performance of your duties. . . . It is not right that men who came here to protect you and me should be thus attacked.[77]

But even while the jurors were assured of protection by those gentle souls whose name has spelled terror in the Pennsylvania coal fields from their beginning to this day, they were also assured that if they acquitted Doyle the operators' vigilantes would see that "justice is done."

"If you disregard such testimony," the General said, "you would be hooted and driven from the community." And: "If they [the jurymen] do not return a verdict of guilty in this case, it would result in the formation of vigilance committees and a resort to 'Lynch Law.' " [78]

The presiding judge allowed all such threats to be made without interference. Every time the defense attempted to protest against the introduction of "isms" which had nothing to do with the charge of murder, the objection was over-ruled. It was not Doyle who was tried, but the whole labor movement, not only in the anthracite fields but throughout the country. Already, in every industrial area, the name of Molly Maguire was attached to the first sign of militancy.

On February 1, the Doyle case went to the jury, with the *Daily Miners' Journal* confident of a result favorable to the operators:

> At about 5 o'clock the jury retired. The general expectation was that no great amount of time would be required for them to arrive at the verdict, which had seemed inevitable, that of conviction of murder in the first degree.

Nevertheless the verdict was delayed. The jurors battled all night and the rumor spread that a single juryman stood for an acquittal. "The supposed refractory juryman," said the *Journal,* "came in for a great deal of public condemnation."

Finally the jury returned to the box bringing a verdict: "Guilty of murder in the first degree."

"The people of anthracite Pennsylvania," said the *Journal,* "will breathe free to-day because of the verdict delivered yesterday in the Doyle trial at Mauch Chunk. For

once the influence of the Molly Maguires has been broken.
. . . The jury must have credit for bravery (*sic!*) and
conscientious uprightness. . . . We congratulate Carbon
County on the skill of her lawyers and the pluck of her
jurymen." The article continued with the hope that the
state would, by further prosecutions, destroy the miners'
organization completely, "especially if it vigorously follows
up in the subsequent cases, as we hope it will." [79]

The hope of the *Miners' Journal* was fulfilled. Kelly
and Alexander Campbell were swiftly tried and as swiftly
condemned to death and all over the anthracite country
mine leaders were being arrested for this and that murder
and swiftly sentenced to hang.

At Tamaqua on July 6, 1875, a policeman named Benjamin F. Yost had been shot and killed. He had left his
home at two o'clock in the morning to make his rounds. It
was a part of his duty to extinguish the night-lamps with
which the town was lighted; and as he stepped onto a lad-
der to reach a high post he was shot, dying the next morning. Every effort was made to discover his assailant or
assailants. He himself, as his wife later testified, did not
know who they were:

I said: "Frank, do you know who shot you?" and he said, "No,
but there was two Irishmen—one smaller than the other." Then
McCarron came and I took hold of him and said, "Do you know
who did it," but he gave me no answer.[80]

It is important to remember this in the light of future
developments. For, when six months had passed five arrests were suddenly made; and the state undertook to show,
not only that they had known the supposed murderers' guilt
from the beginning, but that they could convict them from
Yost's own deathbed statements.

One of the arrested was James Carroll, American born

of Irish miner parents. He was the active manager of the Tamaqua branch of the Ancient Order of Hibernians, a married man of about forty years of age, the father of four children and well thought of in his community.

McParlan, active in this case as well as the previous ones, charged that the murder of Yost had been planned in Carroll's saloon by the Hibernians at whose head he was.

Four other men were arrested. Thomas Duffy, a younger man, was a militant worker employed as engineer at the Buckville Colliery of the Philadelphia and Reading Coal and Iron Company. He was supposed to have put up $10.00 to pay the men who actually did the shooting. James Roarity had come to this country from Ireland in 1869. After working for a few months in the furnaces at Allentown, he had taken his wife and gone into the Lehigh and Wilkes-Barre Coal Company mines at Coaldale. He was supposed to have loaned his pistol for use in Yost's murder. The actual shooting, the prosecution claimed, was done by two men, Hugh McGeehan, a young Irish miner who had been blacklisted for his activities during the Long Strike of 1875, and James Boyle, an American who for five years before his arrest had been employed at the No. 5 Colliery in the Panther Creek Valley.

The Yost case was the first in which Gowen actually appeared in court against the A. O. H. Counsel for the prosecution also included, again, General Albright.

The trial began in May, three months after the men were arrested and nine after the actual killing. Before it could be finished, however, one of the jurors died and not until a year after Yost's death, in July, 1876, was a new jury impaneled and the second trial begun. In the meantime Duffy had requested and been granted a separate trial, but the other four—the two accused of the actual shooting, and

Carroll and Roarity, implicated as active members of the Hibernians—were tried together.

At this trial the chief witness beside McParlan was the very Kerrigan who had been arrested for the murder of Jones and turned state's evidence. He was still under indictment for the Jones affair. It is clear that he had to choose between a noose for himself and freedom at the price of the other miners' deaths. He chose the latter.

Kerrigan, though he was to have somewhat the reputation of a hero for his part in the conviction of the mine leaders, was certainly no savory character. He was an habitual drunkard. Even in such a book as the *Lives and Crimes of the Molly Maguires,* certainly in bitter opposition to the Hibernians, we find this characterization:

> Kerrigan is of all the others the man who did most to corrupt the trade societies of the coal regions, but by "squealing" he saved his own life. He is by nature a thoroughgoing loafer and scoundrel, without a single redeeming trait, while others, if without excuse for their crimes, had some kind of reason for their criminality. McGeehan had been "blacklisted," and he sought to punish with death the man who had deprived him of work. The others were in active sympathy with him because some day his fate might be theirs. Kerrigan alone was without any palliation, except the drunken malevolence of an evil nature. He was criminal because from his very birth he was prone to crime.[81]

Nevertheless the state used this man as a witness; the court accepted his testimony; the jury believed what he said—or if they did not behaved as if they did. McParlan succeeded in making of Kerrigan what he tried to make of Harry Orchard thirty years later during the trial of William D. Haywood.

Kerrigan told the court that the shooting of Yost to his certain knowledge had been planned by the officials of the

Ancient Order of Hibernians, that he was present when McGeehan fired the fatal shot, and that Boyle was also there. Or rather, he actually told nothing, merely confirming with a simple affirmation every detail as McParlan related it.

At any rate the testimony was effective. It condemned McGeehan and Boyle to death. At the beginning of the trial George B. Kaercher, of the prosecution's counsel, had promised, in spite of Mrs. Yost's statements, to convict the defendants by Yost's own words.

"Yost said that he was shot, that he was dying, and that he must die; and that these declarations he repeated many times over during the night and narrated the circumstances of the shooting and who had shot him and all who participated in the shooting so far as he could tell anything about it." [82] But when the time came to show these declarations, they could not be produced.

The defense had made a point of Kerrigan's character and reputation and insisted further that he could not be admitted as a witness because if his story were true he was himself an accomplice to the crime. The prosecution, however, demanded of the jury that it should consider, not "how bad Kerrigan is," or "how many times he assisted in the perpetration of murder or of arson," but only that he was on the "right" side.[83] And the court upheld the prosecution.

The defense then charged that Kerrigan was not only an accomplice to the murder, as he himself admitted, but the actual killer. Testimony by Dr. F. S. Solliday, who attended the policeman before his death, from Daniel Schepp, a friend of Yost, and from Kerrigan's own wife, does much to support this charge.

Dr. Solliday testified that he had heard Yost warn his friend McCarron in these words: " 'Be careful of Kerrigan,' says he, 'they will have you yet, the same as they have me.' " [84]   And what follows is taken from Schepp's testimony. Schepp was asked:

You said that Yost and Kerrigan had considerable difficulty, and Yost arrested him several times. How often do you know that he arrested him?

I cannot mention the number of times, but I think half a dozen at least.

Do you know that Yost was in apprehension that Kerrigan would take his life?

Yost always told me, in connection with this, that he was afraid of those two—Kerrigan and Duffy; he always put them together; he told me that six or eight times. [85]

Mrs. Kerrigan's testimony was perhaps the most startling and important introduced by any single individual during the trials. Drab and miserable, in terror of her husband, and yet somehow fierce and even noble, she stood on the witness stand, to charge her husband with "the crime of Yost" and to declare that he was trying to send innocent men to the gallows to save his own hide. What is printed below is taken verbatim from the court records:

Q. Was your husband the owner of a pistol? A. Yes sir.

Q. About how long had he owned the pistol? A. I think about one year.

Q. What did your husband do after he came? After you let him in? A. After I let him in?

Q. Yes. A. Why, he had his boots in his hand when I let him in, and he said he shot Yost.

Gowen took Mrs. Kerrigan under cross-examination, and the following testimony took place:

Q. You have never been to see your husband since that time, have you? A. No, sir.

Q. Have you refused to send him clothes? A. Yes, sir.

Q. And do anything for him? A. Yes, sir.

Q. Did you not come down to Pottsville, voluntarily, and of your own will, some time ago to make a statement or affidavit that your husband had killed Yost; did you not do that of your own motive? A. I made my statement before I came to Pottsville.

Q. You made it before Squire O'Brien? A. Yes.

Q. You went there voluntarily? A. Of my own accord.

Q. To get your husband hung? A. To tell the truth.

Q. To have the father of your children hung? A. Not when I was telling the truth.

Q. Why did you not send him his clothes when he was lying in prison? A. Why, because he picked innocent men to suffer for his crime.

Q. Because he picked up innocent men to suffer for his crime? A. Yes, sir.

Q. Why did you refuse to go and see him when he had sent word that he wanted to see you? A. Because any man that does such a crime that he done, why should I turn around then, and——

Q. And what; go on. A. That is all.

Q. What crime had he done? A. What crime did he do?

Q. Yes. A. The crime of Yost.

Q. The murder of Yost? A. Yes, sir.[86]

To identify McGeehan and Boyle the prosecution brought in McGeehan's landlady, Mrs. Burns, "a woman of bad reputation"; and one Robert Brislin, who testified that early in the morning of July 6 he had met the two men on an out-of-the-way path near his father's house, and that they had told him they were returning from a ball at Mauch Chunk. His evidence, which hardly seems very conclusive on its face, was, however, discredited when the defense charged, and he himself admitted, that it was being paid for by the Lehigh and Wilkes-Barre Co., with the promise of a position as mine-boss. Mrs. Burns testified that Mc-Geehan had come home after daylight on the morning of the murder and told her that he had been at Summit Hill and Nesquehoning. It must be noted, though, that in May at the first unfinished trial, this same woman had testified that her boarder had been home all of the night that Yost was shot.

This she cleared up—to the satisfaction of the prosecutor and the court—with the statement that she had given false testimony at the first trial but that her priest had now "convinced her to tell the truth."

Two of Boyle's relatives had sworn an alibi for him. They were promptly arrested and convicted of perjury. (We have already noted that no such charge was brought against the "eye-witnesses" who testified for the prosecution in the Dougherty case, though the falseness of their testimony had finally been admitted by the court.)

And how of Roarity? The prosecution speaks: "You have in evidence, as I have already stated, that Roarity was a Molly Maguire; you have it in evidence that upon the 5th of July he was in Tamaqua." [87] On this statement the prosecution asked for—and received—his conviction and death. Before this Gowen had declared that the words "Molly Maguire" attached to a man's name were sufficient to hang him.

Roarity, we remember, was formally charged with having become an accomplice to the murder by loaning the fatal pistol to McGeehan. The gun was one supposed, at some previous time, to have been given to a man named E. B. Whitenight for repair. Whitenight indeed testified that he had repaired one which he thought resembled that shown in court.

We produce proof that this pistol was in the possession of White-night for repair, and that one of the men who came for it was Alexander Campbell, he thinks, and the other man was a man with dark hair. Please, look at Roarity. There is no one of the defendants who has darker hair than Roarity. The probability is that Roarity and Campbell came for the pistol.[88]

The proof offered, however, was very dubious. Not only did Whitenight fail to positively identify the pistol, but definitely stated that he could not recognize any of the men on trial as having brought it to him for repair or taken it back from him. The question was put to him directly: "Do you know James Roarity, here, one of the prisoners, by sight?"

"No," the identifying witness answered. "No, I do not think I do." [89]

On no more solid steps than these—reputed membership in the Hibernians, the accident of dark hair instead of light, the word of a lady whose opinions on facts changed almost from day to day—Roarity and his associates were being led to the gallows, never for murder, but for threatening the operators' profits.

Carroll was accused of no more than having owned the hotel in which the murder was supposed to have been planned, and which was known as a headquarters of the Hibernians, of whom he was a leader. He died on the gallows for that.

The coal operators were determined to crush the miners' organizations—first the union, then the remnants which survived in the Ancient Order of Hibernians. As was the case in the Doyle trial, General Albright frankly and openly made an appeal to the property interests and fears of the jurors. In his summing up before the Jury he said:

It is almost inconceivable how this bad society has injured you and every property-owner in the coal regions. Perhaps there is no portion of our country richer than the anthracite region, and because we live right in the midst of it we forget the surroundings of marvelous wealth. I suppose I do not exaggerate when I say that probably there are a hundred millions of dollars invested directly and indirectly in Schuylkill County pertaining to the coal business alone, embracing, of course, the railroads and canal, and all built and projected for the purpose of getting at the rich treasure underlying the surface of the earth. . . . The money invested in coal property, in railroads and transporting companies which are arteries of this great business amounts to about 350 or 400 million of dollars.

It is a fact that not over one-third of the capital so invested in these times receives any remuneration. When you take into consideration the further fact that capital is naturally conservative, and then, when you find these enterprises confronted by a body of men who seek to control the coal mines and capital invested in them, who, when fancying themselves injured, strike down a mining-boss or police-officer, who endeavored faithfully to discharge his duties, you can see how capital, how property, how life, how everything have been imperiled, and how men of families, and who love them, too, become alarmed, and feel they dare no longer remain in the region, but leave and give place to inferior men, and, in consequence, the business of this particular community was about being surrendered to lawless and desperate men, when, by a train of providences, these murderers and assassins were brought to the front, and some of them are now in *this* front, in your presence, and you are to pass judgment upon them.[90]

We could hardly ask for a more open and brutal statement.

Duffy was tried separately and, like the others, sentenced to die for Yost's murder. Only Kerrigan who, there is much reason to believe, was the actual murderer, went free. In all other Molly Maguire cases the prosecution could contend that miners killed mine-bosses and superintendents to avenge economic grievances. Here there was not even that to account for the conspiracy to shoot Yost. There was no apparent motive for the murder by the five who died for it; proof of their guilt hardly entered the case. They were convicted of membership in the A. O. H. Their death was a part of the operators' plan to destroy all workers' organizations in the coal fields.

Even Reverend McDermott, one of the very Catholic priests who had denounced the Hibernians and who later attended Carroll and Duffy in prison had to declare that: "I know, beyond all reasonable doubt, that Duffy was not a party to the murder of Policeman Yost, and I think the same remark will apply with almost equal force to Carroll." [91]

On the platform before the gallows Carroll and Roarity, as well as the others, professed their innocence to the last moment.

CHAPTER VII

THE TRIALS (*Continued*)

It is impossible to say now how many men died as Molly
Maguires. For two years there was a veritable terror that
fell wherever a miner lifted his head in leadership above
his fellows. During this period wages in the pits were
steadily falling, the hours of work increasing and conditions
of health and safety growing progressively worse. Terror
kept many from protesting; where there was protest it must
be fierce and secret. And fierce was the revenge of the operators and the courts which they controlled. The cases in
which, as Gowen held, hanging was justified by mere membership in the A. O. H., became so common that the records
of many sank into obscurity. Only when they were particularly striking did they arouse general attention. Many
have disappeared from view altogether.

But among the cases which did attract wide attention
was that of Thomas Munley, reported extensively in the
operators' own paper, the *Daily Miners' Journal*. The trial
is particularly remembered for a speech delivered by Gowen
as chief prosecutor, given widespread publication at the time
and still available.

Munley had come to Pennsylvania from Ireland in 1864,
when he was only nineteen years of age. Six years later he
was married and settled at Gilberton in the anthracite.
He became active in the Shenandoah division of the Hibernians and, apparently, a thorn in the mine owners' side.
For a long time, however, nothing could be found against
him.

Then, on September 1, 1875, at Raven Run, a breaker boss by the name of Thomas Sanger and a friend of his known as Uren were attacked and killed. Later McParlan, who was active in this case, would contend, as he had before, that he had not only known at the time who committed the crime, but even that he had been aware of it in advance as a project.

As a matter of fact, no arrests were made for five months. Then, on February 10, 1876, Thomas Munley and Charles McAllister were arrested and charged with the murder of Sanger and Uren. The men, it was charged, were attacked and killed by five men, Munley and Charles McAllister, Michael Doyle (not the Michael J. Doyle hanged for shooting Jones), and two brothers named O'Donnell. Munley was supposed to have been the actual murderer of Sanger.

McAllister asked for and received a separate trial, and on June 27, 1876, at Pottsville, the Munley trial opened. Gowen acted as chief counsel for the Commonwealth, and McParlan its chief witness.

Neither Michael Doyle nor Thomas Hurley, who was also involved in this case, were ever arrested. Nor were they brought as witnesses. The defense charged that McParlan had purposely permitted them to escape, to which Gowen replied: "Pinkerton's Agency may sometimes permit a man to believe that he is free, who does not know that he may be traveling five thousand miles in the company of those whose vigilance never slumbers and whose eyes are never closed in sleep." [92]   But if this is true, then the ghosts of Michael Doyle and Thomas Hurley must still be traveling, still in the erroneous belief that they are free, and in the company of the unwearied and sleepless spirit of a Pinkerton, for they were never heard of again.

In the Munley trial the prosecution was to prove, chiefly on the testimony of McParlan, the charge of conspiracy to murder. Gowen himself could make no more convincing case of it than this, taken from his summary:

On the morning of the 31st of August, McParlan, who had slept the night before with Michael Doyle, was informed by him that he with some others were going to shoot a boss at Raven Run. Doyle wanted one of his [McParlan's] coats, and got it; and Thomas Hurley then came in and instructed Doyle how he should perform his murderous work. After that, this man Hurley remained with McParlan the whole of the day, so as to prevent him from communicating with any one; and on the next morning at eight o'clock, immediately after the perpetration of the crime, panting with the speed of the flight and reeking with the blood of their victims, the five assassins rushed into the house of Michael Lawlor at Shenandoah, and into the presence of Hurley and McParlan himself.

These men announced at once, that they had killed a man, that they had killed a boss, that they had intended to kill only one, but they had to kill another. They said that they did not intend to kill more than one, but the other man interfered and they killed him, too; and then each recounted the share which he had taken in the exploit. Munley specifically related the position which he occupied and the part he had taken in the murder. . . .[93]

We are asked to believe, then, that the very men who did not trust McParlan, according to his own testimony having kept him under Hurley's watch so that he could not communicate with any one, then naïvely came to him and gave him a detailed account of a murder that they had committed, and of their own parts in it. We must also be prepared to believe that McParlan, having full information of the murder, chose to wait for five months to reveal it. In the interim, as we have related before, a masked mob had attacked the house in Wiggan's Patch where the O'Donnell brothers and the McAllister brothers lived. Charles O'Donnell was killed. The other men escaped, the remaining O'Donnell disappeared from the country, and Munley and

Charles McAllister remained at work in the pits until their arrest.

In the Munley case a number of alleged eye-witnesses were introduced by the prosecution. But even if we allow for the tricks which time plays on memory, there is enough divergence and contradiction in their stories to make them all incredible.

Robert Heaton, a partner in the company which employed Sanger, declared that while eating his breakfast on the morning of the murder he heard shots and rushed outside. "On his way to the scene of the murder," said Gowen, "he met his superintendent, wounded and bleeding, and believing, as he struggled into Mr. Weevil's house, that he was about to die, this brave superintendent, who died at his post, uttered his last words to his employer: 'Never mind me, give it to them, Bob.'"

Hearing which, still according to Gowen, Heaton rushed after the murderers who were retreating up the road "three in front and two behind. He shot at the retreating fugitives. The two that were behind turned upon him and faced him directly, so that they were face to face." Heaton added that while on his way to breakfast that morning he had seen some men sitting on a fence some five hundred feet away from him and that "one of these men sat in a peculiar and apparently constrained position."[94]

At a hearing on a writ of *habeas corpus* some months before the trial Heaton came into the courtroom and "was attracted by one of the prisoners sitting in the Court in the same peculiar constrained position." With unerring logic he and the prosecution—and the court—deduced that no two men could conceivably sit in "a peculiar constrained position." The man on the fence became Munley, the man in court; and, by the same token, Heaton an "eye-witness" to the murder.

Gowen said that Heaton had met the murderers "face to face," the face in this case being a man's shoulders, seen three city blocks away.

But, said Gowen: "Of what avail is it that we did not ask the witness whether he recognized this prisoner by his face or not, because the necessary and inevitable inference from what he said is that he did recognize him by his face." [95] And from this "necessary and inevitable inference" Munley was to be hanged.

Gowen, we have just noted, described Sanger as "struggling into Mr. Weevil's house." Yet, only a few minutes before, and in the same speech, the mine owner-prosecutor had described the killing somewhat differently:

This man [Sanger] was confronted by one of an armed band of five assassins. He was shot in the arm. He turned to run around a house in the neighborhood, and he was there confronted by another of these miscreants who had been sent to intercept him. He again turned and stumbled upon the ground; and then, when the foremost of this band of assassins came upon him, as he lay upon the ground, he [the assassin] discharged his revolver into him, and another turned him, as he lay upon his face, over upon his back, so that he could expose a deadly part for his aim, and then, with calm deliberation, selected a vital spot and shot him as he lay prostrated upon the ground.[96]

Mrs. Janey Williams was another identification witness. Gowen summarized her testimony as follows: When a shot was heard, her son rushed for the door to see what had happened. Mrs. Williams and her daughter followed him, and Mrs. Williams, "throwing her arms around his neck at the front door, strove with all her strength and with additional assistance of her daughter and another, to force him from the path of the murderer. When so engaged, with all the dread of the danger before her, she sees one of the murderers pass the door, with his head defiantly in the air, and with his pistol in his hands." [97]

Mrs. Williams' son, however, contradicted her testimony in several important points. While she had been struggling with him at the front door, he, with equal vigor, had struggled with her at the *back* door. And front door or back, he was positive that he had called for no gun.

Moreover, Mrs. Williams' identification was not very positive, to say the least.

"Did you have a view of the man's face?" she was asked.

"I had a side view."

"Is that," indicating Munley, "the man?"

"I had just a side view of him; I could not tell by the front view, but the side view looks like the man."

The defense protested that after the very fleeting sight to which Mrs. Williams confessed, she could not in reason have had any very clear idea of the features she had seen. To which Mr. Gowen replied:

There are authentic instances of detection even in less time. The dog of a murdered man saw an assassin in the act of murder, and that one glimpse lasted for days and weeks and months . . . There are mechanical appliances that render identification instantaneous. The art of the photographer has discovered a method whereby, in an instant of time or less than an instant, in a pulsation of the heart, in a winking of an eye, you can take the picture of a man while he is moving at full speed before you. Why should not the eye of this woman be able to do the same thing? [98]

Why, indeed!

Mrs. Williams also said that: "It seems to me that I could always see that face." (Side view and with reservations, we must presume.) But the identification was accepted.

If any one could have identified Munley it should have

been Richard Andrews. He had, he said, been walking
with Sanger and Uren when suddenly a man came up and
began to shoot. He ran around Weevil's house to escape
the bullets, but soon returned to care for Sanger. He
"went around to Weevil's house and saw him [Sanger]
sitting on the floor. . . . He was wounded and sitting in
Weevil's house."

Andrews gave a detailed description of the murderer.
Here is his testimony:

> Did you see his face?
> I saw his face.
> How was his face as to whiskers?
> He had a mustache; a small mustache.
> Can you tell the color of his hair or eyes?
> No, sir; I cannot.
> Had you ever seen that man before?
> I never saw that man before that morning.
> Did you know him at all?
> No, I did not know him at all.
> Have you ever seen him since?
> Yes, sir.
> Munley, stand up. Is that the man?
> *That is not the man that I can recognize at all.*[99]

This was a bombshell thrown at the prosecution. If there
was any reason for supposing that Munley was really being
tried for murder, that his trial was anything less than a
frame-up, or that his fate was not ordained in advance,
then this should have been fatal to Gowen's case. It was
not.

Nor were these the only contradictions among the state's
witnesses. Andrews said that the murderer wore a "hat."
Mrs. Williams insisted that he had a "cap." Heaton, again,
had seen a "hat," but Arnold stood for the "cap." Andrews
said the assassin had a mustache; but Mrs. Williams testi-

fied: "No, sir; he had none. No, sir; I did not notice any." [100]

The defense also brought in witnesses who had rushed outside and they heard the shot that killed Sanger. Men who had known Munley for years testified that he was not in the attacking group. Other defense witnesses established an alibi for him. But nothing availed. In every case the witness was asked whether he or she belonged to or sympathized with or had anything at all to do with the Ancient Order of Hibernians. If so, then that was sufficient proof of lying and perjury. Such was the attitude of the prosecution; and both judge and jury were quite ready to believe that any man or woman who testified for the defense was, *per se*, a lying scoundrel. The proof of murder was thin and weak. The evidence that Munley was an active and militant member of the miners' organizations was overwhelming. And that, we remember, was "enough to hang any man." It hanged Munley and his fellow Hibernians.

In his last speech, L'Velle, of the defense attorneys, made it plain that it was not individuals who were being tried, but the working class in the mine fields.

"For God's sake," he cried, "give labor an equal chance. Do not crush it. Let it not perish under the imperial mandates of capital in a free country." [101]

It was rather a nice prayer as prayers go, but apparently it went unheard in heaven, and it was certainly disregarded by the judge and the jury whose place it was to follow the lead of coal-company-president-prosecutor Gowen, who frankly appealed to the jurymen to do their job as property-holders:

Of what use would capital or wealth, or industry, or enterprise, or protection amount to, if the administration of the resources of this county and the development of its wealth were intrusted to those who went to do their duty, dogged by the assassin and the murderer, unknowing whether, when they left their houses in the morning, they would not be carried back dead before night? . . .

But, at last, the ruling class is safe, private property rules supreme. "We can stand up before the whole country," continues Gowen, "and say, 'Now all are safe in this country; come here with your money; come here with your enterprises; come here with your families and make this country your residence; help us to build up this people and you will be safe.'" And, finally, stretching his arms to the jury, Gowen foams and threatens:

I believe I have done my duty; for God's sake, let me beg of you do not shrink from doing yours. Solemn judges of the law and of the facts—august ministers in the temple of justice—robed for sacrifice, I bring before you this prisoner and lay him upon your altar . . . and *trembling at the momentous issues involved in your answer,* I ask you, will you let him go? [102]

The presiding judge instructed the jury that it should give less weight to the testimony of the defense than to that of the prosecution because, forsooth, the former was "negative" and the latter "positive." "You will readily see," he said, "that it is not entitled to the same weight as the positive evidence of witnesses who swear they saw him." [103]

And the jurymen, Gowen's "august ministers, robed for the sacrifice," found Thomas Munley "guilty of murder in the first degree." [104] He was sentenced to death on the gallows.

Charles McAllister was never brought to trial for the murder of Sanger and Uren. Instead the charge was transferred to his brother, James, who had in the meantime disappeared. Later, Charles was indicted, tried and imprisoned for the "attempted assassination" of James Riles of Shenandoah.

During the years of 1876 and 1877 the trials increased in frequency and viciousness.

How intimately the trials were bound to the struggle is easily seen from a number of features common to nearly all of them. When men who were not members of the Hibernians or known to be inactive in the struggle were included among the defendants, they were freed or allowed to escape. In a number of the cases the crimes for which the Hibernians were tried were very old, apparently being brought to light at moments convenient to the operators. And in every case, it was enough to prove a man a member of the A. O. H. to hang him.

John Kehoe, Schuylkill County delegate of the Ancient Order of Hibernians, was widely known as a fearless leader of the miners. He was a bold and outstanding fighter; the work of breaking the A. O. H. in the anthracite counties could not be completed so long as he was at large. In August, 1876, he and eight other men, all Hibernians, were brought to trial and later imprisoned for conspiracy to kill one William M. Thomas, wounded by gunshot at Mahonoy City some fifteen months before.[105] Here, as he had before, McParlan claimed full advance knowledge of the crime.

The conspiracy charge was successfully sustained in this case and Kehoe sent to jail. But the imprisonment of Kehoe did not satisfy the prosecution. Immediately upon the completion of this trial Kehoe was again tried with several others for conspiracy to kill Jesse and Williams Major, though neither man had been attacked. Finally, in November, 1876, he was taken from jail to be tried and sentenced to death as having been one of a group responsible for the death of F. W. S. Langdon.

The charge dated back fourteen years, to June 14, 1862, when Langdon, a breaker boss, heartily disliked among the men he aided in exploiting, had been stoned by a crowd. He did not die immediately. The day after the stoning he felt "pretty good and walked to his home about a mile distant." Three days afterward, however, he died, supposedly from wounds received at the hands of the crowd. Now, after all these years, Kehoe was charged with being "present when the concerted effort was made and the numerous and repeated blows were given." [106] It will be noted that he was not even accused of having actually struck Langdon. Yet the jury found him "guilty in the first degree of murder" and the court sentenced him to death.

An appeal was rejected by the Supreme Court of the State of Pennsylvania, and Kehoe was rushed to the scaffold from which he delivered these words, the last he spoke: "I am not guilty of the murder of Langdon: I never saw the crime committed." [107]

The last trial which we shall consider here is perhaps the most high-handed and brutal of them all. Patrick Hester, Peter McHugh and Patrick Tully were found guilty and were rushed to the gallows. These were the circumstances:

On October 17, 1868, Alexander W. Rea, a mining superintendent of Centralia, Columbia County, was murdered and in December of the same year, Patrick Hester, Thomas Donahue, Michel Prior and John Duffy, were arrested and charged with his death. Donahue was tried February 2-11, 1869, and found not guilty. On May 5, 1869, Duffy went on trial with the same result. Prior's trial took place May 11, and he, too, was acquitted. Hester had remained in jail and demanded a trial. But the government refused to try him, and on the day Duffy was freed he, too, was discharged.

The murder was forgotten for over seven years. But

Hester was a very influential man among the miners. And by 1876 the coal interests were set in their determination to destroy the miners' organization by murdering their leaders. Hester was a Body-Master of the A. O. H.; therefore he, too, must be put out of the way. McHugh was a county delegate of the A. O. H. Tully was an active, militant fighter. They, too, must go. Therefore, early in 1877, all were arrested. There was no new crime to attach to them, and they were charged with the old murder of Rea.

Hester entered a special plea on the ground that his indictment on this charge had already been dismissed by the court in 1869, and that he could not be prosecuted a second time for the same alleged crime. But his plea was rejected.

On February 8, 1877, a jury was sworn in at Bloomsburg, Pa.; on February 24 they were found "guilty of murder in the first degree." On May 10, a motion for a new trial was overruled, and four days later the defendants were sentenced to death. It was a quick and efficient job. Just how was it accomplished?

"After seven years have passed," we read in the introduction of the trial records, "on confession of Manus Cull, alias Daniel Kelly, one of the most abandoned criminals, the confessed murderer of Rea, the defendants, Tully and McHugh, were arrrested as participants in the murder, and Hester was rearrested as an accessory before the fact." [108]

Further on, the same writer says again:

The principal witness in this case, and without whose testimony there could have been a conviction of neither of the defendants, was Manus Cull, alias Daniel Kelly. He admitted himself on the witness stand to be the most abandoned, degraded and heartless criminal. Not only did he confess that he murdered and robbed Rea, but that he had at different times been guilty of every crime known to the criminal law. He was scarcely out of prison for one offense until he was sent back for another. He was in prison in Schulykill

County serving out a 10-year term for robbery. He had some difficulty with his fellow prisoners, as a result of which he learned that he was not merely suspected of the murder of Rea, but that there were parties in the same prison who knew it, and he had reason to believe that when his term expired he would be tried and convicted of the offense.

Under these circumstances, through the manipulations of the detectives, he made a statement to them in which Tully and McHugh were charged with being actual participants in the murder, and Patrick Hester was implicated as an accessory before the fact. He was irregularly pardoned, as contended by the defendants, to make him a witness. He was confessedly infamous, and was brought from the prison where he was under sentence for highway robbery, and under inoperative pardon was allowed to testify. He was the principal witness, and on his testimony the defendants were convicted. No one can read his testimony without being shocked at the criminal and pronouncing him too infamous to be worthy of belief.

Yet he was allowed under objections to testify to circumstances entirely unconnected with this case, to acts of his own, in the absence of the prisoners with which they had no connection, merely for the purpose of corroborating himself. He contradicted himself; was contradicted by a number of reliable witnesses, and his general character for truth and veracity was most thoroughly impeached. The defendants' counsel contended that he was so thoroughly discredited by his own admissions and all the evidence in this case, that it was the plain duty of the court to direct the jury to disregard his testimony.[109]

During the trial, a correspondent of the *New York Herald* sent an item from Bloomsburg, dated February 19, 1877, which also shows how Cull, or Kelly, was regarded:

An army of witnesses has been summoned here from Schuylkill, Carbon, Northumberland and Luzerne counties to bear testimony to the fearful character of "Kelly the Bum," the principal prop of the prosecution in the trial of Hester, Tully, and McHugh for the murder of Alexander Rea, and today no fewer than twenty of them occupied the stand. The majority of those called upon to speak of Kelly's reputation painted it in black and repelling colors enough, but not one-half as black as he himself has already admitted it to be upon the witness stand, so that their statements thus far merely go to corroborate the Molly Maguire informer's own admission. About a dozen men have sworn today that they would not believe Kelly under oath; and if their statements be true he must be one of the most consummate perjurers that ever kissed a book.

Even the state's own witnesses contradicted him, and the defense brought in twenty-five reputable persons who proved him—as he himself confessed to be—a criminal, and a scoundrel who made his whole livelihood from crime. One of the defense witnesses was Benjamin Thomas who had been in jail on a divorce charge while Cull was incarcerated there for robbery. He took the stand to tell of a conversation during which Cull had said:

I would squeal on Jesus Christ if I got out of here. I care no more than that for an oath and care no more than that for it. . . . Hester was accused of the murder of Rea, but, Ben, between you and me, Hester is innocent and knew nothing more about it than you did. . . . And he [Cull] stated that the party that committed murder went into the bush near Hester's house to drink; that in case they were seen there it would naturally be supposed that Hester was to be blamed for it.

And again:

He said he was tired of being in the cell for 19 months, to be confined there, and he said that to get out of there he would swear on Jesus Christ.[110]

Cull's story on the witness stand was that:

the robbery and murder of Rea was planned on the night of October 16, 1868, at the saloon of Thomas Donahue in Ashland, at the suggestion of Patrick Hester; that there were present at the conspiracy ten persons, namely: Patrick Hester, Peter McHugh, Patrick Tully, Ned Skiffington, Brian Campbell, James Bradley, William Muldooney, Roger Lafferty, Jack Dalton, and himself; that its object was money.[111]

The defense put up many witnesses who gave alibis for the defendants. Six witnesses—Fahey, Richardson, Britt, McLaughlin, Luby and Casey—definitely testified that Hester was, at the time the crime was committed, in another place. Sworn affidavits were also filed with the court by the defense. But, as in other cases, the question was not the guilt or innocence of the defendants, but that they were leaders of the A. O. H. The non-Hibernians named by Cull were, apparently, never brought to trial.

Cull was well rewarded by the government of the coal operators. In return for his agreement to incriminate the innocent leaders of the Ancient Order of Hibernians he was released from jail and never brought to trial for the murder to which he confessed.

McParlan also figured in the Hester-Tully-McHugh trial. His rôle in the courtroom was a very simple one. He merely said that Hester was a leader of the Ancient Order of Hibernians—sufficient, as we already know, to hang any man. It hanged Hester.

CHAPTER VIII

"PEACE ONCE MORE REIGNS . . ."

THE performance is nearly ended. Soon the curtain will fall, covering men's faces hooded for the noose, the dangling feet of workers whose crime was the leadership of their fellows. Gowen and the other leading citizens who only two years ago spoke so righteously of the epidemic of crime swearing to stamp it out and, so, to avenge society, have rewarded with freedom men like Kerrigan, Cull and Mulhearn—vicious criminals who achieved sanctity at the cost of other men's deaths.

The official records show nineteen executions; in 1877: Thomas Munley, James Carroll, James Roarity, Hugh McGeehan, James Boyle, Thomas Duffy, Michael J. Doyle, Edward J. Kelly, Alexander Campbell, John Donahue, Thomas P. Fisher, John Kehoe, Patrick Hester, Patrick Tully, Peter McHugh, Peter McManus, and Andrew Lanahan.

Charles Sharpe and James McDonald were hanged at Mauch Chunk on January 14, 1879. In their case a reprieve from the governor was sent—just after they were hanged. There is little doubt that the gesture was deliberate, a shady compromise between the rising tide of protest against the shocking butchery of the executions and the operators' desire to have all the mine leaders out of the way. Even the New York *World*, throughout the trials unfriendly to the miners' cause, felt called upon to offer some form of protest. On January 15, the day after the executions, it said:

116

The double execution at Mauch Chunk yesterday is a disgrace to public justice in the state of Pennsylvania. The demeanor of the men on the scaffold, their resolute and yet quiet protestations of innocence of this crime . . . were things to stagger one's belief in their guilt. . . . They were "Molly Maguires," they were arrested and arraigned at a time of great popular excitement, and they were condemned and hanged "on general principles." . . . The official explanation which is sent from Harrisburg of the delay [of the reprieve] we are sorry to say is rather worse than no explanation at all. . . . What more plausible explanation do the facts themselves suggest than that the Governor of Pennsylvania was willing in deference to one class of his constituents to see the men hanged, while in deference to another class, if for no other reason, he was willing to make a pretense of saving them.

And the *Irish World* for June 16, 1877, writing of the trials of that year:

Now let any man in Pennsylvania, or any man in New York, or any man in the Republic, look at the whole proceedings against those men. Look at the astounding fact that one man confesses to having committed a murder, and then get another man hanged who did *not* commit it; who is not even charged with committing it, who is charged merely with inciting the real murderer to commit the crime. And even that "inciting" sworn to by the criminal himself for the rather tempting reward of getting his own neck out of the halter!

And that was the kind of evidence produced on those trials. We saw no other kind. The men whose lives were thus sworn away were mainly leading intelligent men whose direction gave strength to the resistance of the miners to the inhuman reduction of their wages. What is the reasonable inference? Let the reader who knows Gowen—twenty-thousand-a-year Gowen—and who knows Pershing [one of the judges] and who has watched the Courts and the Juries and the whole proceedings against those ill-fated men— let the reader himself infer the motive that hounds them all on.

Execution of militant miners at Mauch Chunk, Pa. Troops were
present to prevent a rumored attempt at rescue.

These miners were militants. They spoke; they protested; they went on strike and fought against the tyranny of the coal companies; they called on other workers from the mines to wage a common struggle. They were criminals in the eyes of the rulers because they made organized, determined effort to improve their desperately bad conditions.

The trials and executions were, in their day, big news for the press, and vivid descriptions of the hangings were printed throughout the country. One eye-witness of the murder of the miners gave the following picture of the scenes on June 21, 1877:

Time dragged along slowly for the expectant crowd of fully two hundred, waiting in the vicinity of the gallows until long after ten o'clock, the hour at which it was generally expected that the executions would take place. Meanwhile about two thousand persons congregated in the streets without, staring blankly at the jail-walls, and speculating upon the scenes inside. . . .

At fifty-five minutes aften ten o'clock the head of a small procession emerged from the door of the little room . . . and marched down along the brick walk past the new wing of the prison, a distance of about two hundred feet to the gallows. Sheriff Werner marched at the head. Then came McGeehan . . . and Boyle. On each flank walked deputy sheriffs. Behind them was a detachment of the Coal and Iron Police. Boyle carried a huge red rose in his left hand, and frequently raised it to his nose. He also wore a great white rose in a button hole. McGeehan carried in one hand a small brass crucifix, and in the other a little porcelain statuette of the Mother of the Savior. In his button-hole were two big roses, pink and white. . . .

Both men made brief speeches, and were then handcuffed and strapped, while the white caps were being placed over their heads. The nooses were speedily adjusted and the men left standing alone.

The trapdoor on which they stood was pulled from under their feet, and the two bodies dangled in the air. The gallows were cleared and Roarity, Carroll, Duffy and Munley were executed in rapid succession. A priest—as necessary to the hangings as were the Coal and Iron Police—asked Duffy if he had anything to say. He replied with a smile:

"No, there is nothing to say."

"Nothing," assented Munley, calmly.

Edward Kelly, "Yellow Jack" Donahue, Michael J. Doyle and Alexander Campbell were hanged together at Mauch Chunk. The same eye-witness continues:

The town was quiet. Many families, expecting a conflict between the troops and Mollies, had fled from their homes. The militia guarded the neighborhood of the prison, and the Coal and Iron Police were stationed in the jail.

Kelly, Doyle and Donahue were unflinching. Campbell nearly fell on his knees to the floor of the platform, but instantly he recovered self-possession, and was afterwards as firm as the others.[112]

Boyle and McGeehan were hanged together. Boyle turned to his comrade and shouted: "Good-by, old fellow, we'll die like men!" McGeehan nodded his head in approval.

These miners died as working-class heroes always die, head up and unafraid, smiling in the face of their executioners, hurling their inward defiance at those who sent them to the gallows.

The executions were quite diverting to bourgeois society. "A number of young ladies, accompanied by several Presbyterian clergymen from Hazleton and Slatington, were being shown the working of the gallows by a minister of questionable taste." [113]

The joy of the operators over the corpses of their victims was unbounded. It was openly expressed by the owners' press throughout the country. For example, after Alexander

Campbell was sentence to death, the *Daily Miners' Journal,* for July 3, 1876, carried this statement:

The majesty of the law now stands vindicated in the conviction of three of the Thug Fraternity and the visage of justice is doubtless sterner than it ever entered into the heads of the Mollies to imagine.

The Chicago Tribune, in its issue of June 22, 1877, carried an editorial headed: "A Triumph of Law and Justice." It rejoices that the organization of the miners has been shattered, because it "was of abnormal growth. It is a monstrosity such as is seen but once in an age. We need not expect such another in a generation, if indeed ever again."

Dewees also thanked "the energetic and thorough action of the Wilkes-Barre Coal and Iron Company and the Philadelphia and Reading Coal and Iron Company, and the firm attitude maintained by the court and the jury in the discharge of duty." [114]

"Peace once more reigns in the anthracite coal regions," declared Edwards. "Molly Maguirism is practically dead. The inhabitants of the anthracite coal regions are now enjoying the blessed peace which has recently come to them. God rules, justice must reign, and right must triumph." [115]

Stripped of all its verbiage the editorial in the *Miners' Journal* of June 22, 1877, on the day after the executions, reveals the real aim and purpose of the trials and executions. "What did they do?" asks the operators' organ.

"Whenever prices of labor did not suit them they organized and proclaimed a strike."

That was the crime for which the "Molly Maguires" died on the gallows.

CHAPTER IX

CONCLUSIONS

THE first major labor struggle, occurring when conditions were ripening for the rapid development of American capitalism already bore many of the features common to subsequent class battles. During the Civil War period, large-scale industry was already well in the making and the process of the concentration of capital was accelerated. These were the necessary prerequisites for the rule of finance-capital and the development of imperialism. In the Pennsylvania anthracite fields the Civil War hastened the domination of the corporation, and the struggle against the miners was accompanied by the growth of the power of the large-scale coal producing companies. Gowen wielded the power of a coal corporation—with all that it implied in the easy utilization of the powers of the state. For the first time American labor squarely faced this new octopus which was to grow to greater proportions and develop new tentacles with the maturing of imperialism.

In the struggle against the anthracite miners, the employers utilized the greatest array of weapons yet assembled in any American class battle. Paid thugs, the national guard, the labor spy, the press and the courts—the power of propaganda and the power of state—were mobilized against the rebellious workers. Many of these weapons had been pressed into service singly or in less powerful combination in earlier struggles and their rôle as instruments of the ruling class was already evident to a discerning eye. In the battle in the anthracite the labor spy was introduced for the first time according to a well-organized plan. The church had entered into the conspiracy against the miners from the very start. The courts for the first time legalized a wholesale murder of labor leaders.

In this early struggle the operators laid the groundwork for the frame-up system which was to play such an important rôle in the future. Although it is not correct to characterize the trial and execution of the Mollies as a frame-up pure and simple, the frame-up was utilized by the employers to pick off the most militant of the Irish miners in the attempt to terrorize the rest into submission. The execution of the Mollies was the culmination of a class struggle in which the ruling class as victor exterminated its most virulent enemies regardless of the fact whether this individual or that was the actual participant in the killing for which he was convicted. The killings themselves—of which there were more victims among the workers than among the mine owners' entourage—were part and parcel of the fierce class struggle in progress. The operators could paint the miners as assassins and murderers in lurid colors and succeed in giving their characterization a sense of reality because, by the very nature of class society, the press and the state were their instruments.

The Mollies, on their side, were forced to adopt a strategy and tactic new to the labor movement in order to combat the forces brought into play by the operators. Lacking the aid of experiences from any such previous alignment of forces, the Mollies had to explore new terrain for themselves, become pioneers in evolving new methods to fit the new situation. Their background of struggle in Ireland and England stood them in good stead. To them credit must be given for utilizing on a large scale the policy of mass-picketing, of opposing the power of the masses to the concentrated power of the state. The cry, "The miners are on the march!"—which sets the blood tingling in the veins of all class-conscious workers—was experienced as a full-fledged tactic of labor in the anthracite struggle of the seventies. To-day it is a well-established tradition for the miners to march from camp to camp until their strike covers the mine field. When the Western Federation of Miners and the United Mine Workers led their first big strikes the miners were on the march, from one town to another, organizing and swelling the mass picket lines.

When the miners were unsuccessful in stemming the onslaught of the operators and their union was crushed—or at least not permitted to function openly—they carried on their struggle, organizing secretly, seeking out new organizational forms and turning whatever organization at hand into a weapon for their use in the struggle. When the Workmen's Benevolent Association, their union, was crushed, they made the Ancient Order of Hibernians serve them as a struggle organization. They fought to the end. The hangman's noose only succeeded in subduing the open protest until the workers could again gather their forces and, with a background of experience to draw upon, enter into new struggles.

It was inevitable that into this pioneer struggle there should have crept harmful tendencies or that many weaknesses on the part of the workers should have been felt. Undoubtedly, the miners resorted to individual terrorism—though to what degree is hard to tell from the available material. It is evident that some of these murders were committed by provocateurs and Pinkerton agents and later fastened on the miners' leaders. Important it is to note that the killings for which the miners were hanged all took place *before* the Long Strike of 1875, when the operators were using spies and thugs in their attempt to destroy the union and the miners were hard put to it in the defense of their organization and their very lives. During this life and death struggle the miners resorted to a form of guerrila warfare as a method of defending themselves. This right they had—whether they were conscious of it or not—the right of self-defense against unprovoked attacks, a right that every citizen in a democracy was supposed to enjoy. Workers have made use of this right since, in Centralia, Gastonia, and Harlan. To-day the militant labor movement upholds the right of workers to defend themselves against the attacks of the employers' thugs in class battles and proposes the organization of defense corps to beat off lynch mobs.

It was but natural that—faced with the brutal suppression of all their rights, with the murder of their active fellow-workers, with the increased pangs of starvation—individuals among them, lacking class consciousness, should resort to methods of individual terrorism against an especially vicious mine superintendent or mine boss in the period before the strike of 1875 and before the power of mass organization and mass action became evident to them. The miners were subjected to the most bitter exploitation and suffered from an inhuman lack of safety devices in the mines. They were held in feudal bondage by low wages paid in script, exchangeable only at the company stores, and cheated by the coal companies at the scales, for a check-weighman would come only after long years of struggle. At every turn they faced the tyranny of the coal corporations which dominated and governed the whole anthracite territory. That under these conditions certain miners sought to do away with the most vicious of the operators' tools, hoping in this way to relieve their misery, is not to be wondered at. This is a method commonly used by a new proletariat against a new and brutal tyranny.

Only with clearer political insight gleaned from bitter experience, does the working class learn that its struggle is not against this or that individual—who for the moment may typify the system it is fighting—but against the bourgeoisie as a class—a class which exploits and oppresses the vast majority of the people, the toiling masses, and against the state which the bourgeoisie has set up as an instrument with which to oppress the masses. And history has been especially fertile in recent years in producing ample experience of the power that lies in the working class organized as a class, whether it be in a strike or in a revolution. Revolutionary working class leaders have never condemned force as such, but they have rejected individual terrorism for it does not serve the immediate interests of the working class and is prone to harm rather than aid the workers in their struggle.

The weaknesses displayed by the anthracite miners in their struggle were shared by the labor movement as a whole at that time. To expect the workers in the struggles of the seventies to realize and overcome weaknesses that were inherent in the very structure of capitalism at that stage in development and which were necessarily reflected in the labor movement—shortcomings which we can now easily recognize because of the prospective given us by over fifty years of experience—would be to ignore the dialectic process of history. True it was that the Mollies partook of many bourgeois democratic illusions, which were deep-seated in the working class as a whole and for the wiping out of which the situation was not yet ripe. These illusions hampered the miners in their struggle. In the defense of their leaders and fellow-workers they depended primarily upon the accepted procedure of the law courts, resting their faith in a system of justice which, in its essence, could be only class justice. By the time the struggle was over and the militant miners were sentenced to the gallows, there could have been no doubt but that the courts were the instruments of the mine owners in the drive to stamp out the miners' organizations. The miners, their perspectives limited to "legal" defense in the courtroom, failed to carry on the battle for the lives of their fellow-workers by strengthening their struggle at the very pits and by organizing mass defense that would break through the vicious ring of terror and intimidation.

A decisive factor in bringing about the defeat of the miners was their isolation. Here again this was due primarily to the level of development in which the American working class as a whole found itself. Although the self-imposed isolation of the Irish miners, who still suffered from the influence of the Irish nationalist bourgeoisie, undoubtedly played its part, the real cause for their isolation was to be found in the lack of a class-conscious labor movement which recognized any labor struggle, no matter in what part of the country, to be its own.

From the beginning the struggle was restricted to anthracite Pennsylvania. With the exception of one or two of the radical labor papers, themselves isolated from the labor movement, there was no class-conscious working class press to take up the struggle and rally the workers in all parts of the country to the support and defense of the fighting miners. Neither the *Miners' National Record,* the organ of the Miners' National Association, nor the Chicago *Workingmen's Advocate,* the most important labor paper of the time, evidenced much concern over the annihilation of the miners' leaders. The few protest meetings that were held were not powerful enough to make their impress upon the working class.

The official labor movement and its leaders failed to come to the defense of the miners during this life and death struggle in Pennsylvania. Only the revolutionary workers raised their voice of protest against the execution of the militant miners. In larger industrial centers protest mass meetings were held. In Philadelphia the mass meeting protested "against the hasty and inhuman manner in which the so-called 'Molly Maguires' have been sentenced to death." [116]

A mass meeting of workers held at Masonic Hall, in New York City, on January 13, 1877, adopted the following resolution:

Whereas, It is asserted that an organization styled "Molly Maguires" exists in the mining districts "for the purposes of assassination"; *whereas,* this assertion is chiefly based upon the testimony of an infamous person named McParlan, who has been actively engaged in the service of the mine owners; *whereas,* the mining corporations have endeavored to cover with odium the working men of Pennsylvania for the purpose of diverting attention from their own cruel and outrageous robbery of the workmen; be it

Resolved, That this mass meeting of workingmen, in the name of the workingmen of this city, protest against the infamous treatment to which the miners of Pennsylvania are subjected, and the proposed wholesale execution of the men against whom the only testimony was that of hired witness. This meeting further considers it the duty of all workingmen, but more especially those in Pennsylvania, to raise their voice, against the proposed hideous human butchery.[117]

Although faced with such overwhelming condemnation and lack of working class solidarity, the rank and file miners of Pennsylvania stood solidly with their militant leaders who fell as victims in the class war. They raised funds for the defense. They faced the fierce campaigns of terror and intimidation when they testified for the accused miners. Many were sentenced to prison for simply taking the witness stand. Still they fought courageously against the gigantic conspiracy closing in upon their leaders.

It is an eloquent testimonial to the militancy of the rank-and-file miners of the anthracite that during the height of the terror against them they intensified their efforts to save their leaders. The New York *Sun* (June 20, 1877) reported that

The Mollies are by no means defunct. Every little mining village near here [Mauch Chunk] has its organization, and in every place the members have been meeting night after night during the past week with frequency and in numbers such as Maguireism never commanded before.

The retreat of the leaders of the Miners' National Association before the onslaught of the operators and their desertion in the face of the sharpened class struggle in the anthracite, played no little part in dooming the Mollies. The action of the Executive Board of the M.N.A., when the struggle was at its fiercest, in condemning the militant prosecution of the strike by the miners, helped to pave the way for the final slaughter. From the very beginning of the mass organization of labor in this country, opportunism found its expression in the treachery of the labor leaders.

At that time, this opportunism was based on a rapidly developing capitalism, which could, so to speak, buy off certain sections of the workers and their leaders with the profits made from its expanding industries. As American imperialism developed the basis of this opportunism shifted. From the super-profits made in the exploitation of new markets and colonial and semi-colonial peoples, American imperialism corrupted whole sections of the skilled workers and the whole strata of its leadership. Even in face of the militant struggles carried through for the organization of the United Mine Workers of America, its leadership, infected with the virus of opportunism, favored a class collaboration policy as opposed to strike struggles and was forced to lead strikes only by the pressure of a militant rank and file. No strikes were approved by the officials until efforts at bargaining with the operators had failed. Like the officials of the Miners' National Association of the seventies, the bureaucracy of the U.M.W. of A. has failed again and again to call out miners in one field to back a strike elsewhere although this tactic would have been decisive for victory. President John Mitchell pledged his allegiance to Mark Hanna, Republican Party leader and coal operator, and other operators against the miners. When he died he left a fortune of $250,000, largely in coal, railroad, and steel company securities. Many of the U.M.W. of A. officials became coal operators themselves. John L. Lewis is notorious for his autocratic reign in the U.M.W. of A. and his suppression of militant rank-and-filers. William Green received his training in treachery as the secretary-treasurer of the U.M.W. of A. before he became president of the American Federation of Labor, and was Democratic senator in the Ohio state legislature while secretary of the union.

John Boylan, now president of District No. 1 (anthracite Pennsylvania), in his own words gives a perfect characterization of himself and his fellow labor racketeers. The *New York Times* of March 22, 1932, reporting an "unauthorized" strike of anthracite miners against wage-cuts, quotes him as follows:

We stand with the operators against the rebellious elements. We believe in the sanctity of contracts and will carry out our agreement to the letter.

The United Mine Workers of America stands for coöperation with all sane elements in the community to build up the anthracite industry. . . .

Rather than marking the end of any attempts at organization among the miners, the execution of the Mollies in 1877 was followed immediately by more determined efforts at organization. The anthracite miners were joining the Knights of Labor and the miners and laborers of the Lackawanna Coal and Iron Company at Scranton came out during the great railroad strike of 1877. Only two years after the Mollies were hanged another union, the Miners' and Laborers' Amalgamated Association, was attempted in the middle and southern anthracite fields. In 1887, 22,000 miners employed by the Philadelphia and Reading Company, which had carried through the annihilation of the Mollies, struck together with 10,000 men in the Lehigh valley. During this strike, immigrant workers from eastern Europe were used to break the strike and began to replace the Irish and English miners. Through the big strikes of 1900 and 1902 the anthracite miners, many of them new immigrant workers, struck solidly, holding out against the same methods used by the Philadelphia and Reading as had been utilized in the earlier struggles and against the compromise plans of John Mitchell.

The Long Strike of 1875 and the execution of the militant miners were the forerunners to a long series of struggles. Reliance upon mass organization and solidarity won for the workers one demand after another. Beginning with the great railroad strike of 1877, through the struggles led by the Knights of Labor, and the heroic battles of workers in all industries, American labor was achieving organization and victories, although much of this has since been undermined by the reactionary labor leaders.

The fierce battles of the workers for improving their conditions sharpened those weapons which the employers had used against the Mollies. They became an established system in the industrial life of America. The history of the events in the anthracite region in the seventies has been repeated time and again in other industries. In 1886, the struggle for the eight-hour day culminated in the frame-up of the leaders of the Chicago labor movement. The Haymarket martyrs—Spies, Parsons, Fischer and Engel—who were hanged in 1887, were the victims of the class war as Kehoe and his comrades were ten years previously.

Only the organized mass defense of the workers saved Haywood, Pettibone and Moyer—leaders of the militant Western Federation of Miners—from long prison terms on the framed-up charge of murdering ex-Governor Stuenenberg of Idaho. In this case the employers evolved a new weapon—that of kidnaping and carrying their victims to some place where the courts are ready to convict.

The frame-up system, which buried its first permanent roots in the Pennsylvania anthracite, is now murdering by degrees Thomas Mooney and Warren Billings behind California prison bars. They organized the workers in the West and were opposed to plunging the American masses into the world war.

For organizing and leading the lumber jacks in the Northwest and opposing the war, members of the then militant Industrial Workers of the World are in San Quentin prison to-day. They defended themselves and their headquarters against a murderous attack by the American Legion. Eugene V. Debs, was thrust into jail for his opposition to the war as a warning of the ruling class to revolutionary workers against any such activity. The reaction of 1920 ended with the frame-up of Nicola Sacco and Bartolomeo Vanzetti, whose legal murder in 1927 the ruling class hailed as a "vindication of justice," reëchoing the cry of Gowen fifty years before.

The ruthless massacre of workers on strike by thugs, deputies and troops has grown apace with the increased ferocity of the class struggle. Practically every major strike —and even small and isolated ones—add to the record of ruling class murder. Probably in no other so-called civilized country has the ruling class been so brutal in the class war as in the United States. It is only necessary to recall the massacre of nineteen people—miners, their wives and children—by the Baldwin-Felts thugs and state militia serving the Rockefeller interests at Ludlow, Colorado; the wanton shooting, clubbing and beating by thugs and state forces during the great steel, mining, railroad and textile strikes. Of more recent events, we may recall the cold-blooded murder by the Coal and Iron Police of the Pittsburgh Coal Company of John Barkoski in 1929; the murder of six textile strikers by deputies at Marion, N. C., in 1929; the murder of Ella May Wiggins, cotton worker, strike leader and mother of five children, by deputies, during the Gastonia textile strike in the same year; and also in the same year, the murder by police of a number of street-car strikers in New Orleans, La.

The methods used by the miners in their early struggles have since been employed by militant workers. Mass picketing and self-defense are to-day the daily weapons of the workers in their struggles. Virdin Day (October 13, 1898) —when the Illinois miners successfully fought off mine guards and scabs—is still remembered by the miners. The Pinkerton detectives were defeated in good measure by the steel strikers at Homestead, Pa., in 1892, when the Pinkertons attempted to enter the town in a prearranged plan to break the strike. Armed thugs and scabs were given a decisive defeat by the miners of Herrin, Ill., in 1922. Under the leadership of a new union which carried on the militant tradition of American labor, the National Textile Workers' Union, the Gastonia textile strikers in 1929 defended their tent colony from an armed attack by a mob of thugs and police and in the battle the chief of police was shot and killed. Seven strikers and strike leaders were sentenced to long prison terms. Although workers had defended themselves before, this was the first labor case in which the issue of the right of workers' defense was raised sharply and defended by the working class through the International Labor Defense which was in charge of the case.

The end of 1929 marked the beginning of the most deepgoing and fundamental crisis yet experienced by international capitalism. American imperialism, which until then had been able to emerge from its cyclical crises not only regaining lost ground but experiencing a further development, could now only look forward to a process of decay. By 1932 there were twelve million workers totally unemployed in America. The class struggle assumed sharper forms. In place of the corrupted old-line labor bureaucracy a new working class force made a sharp bid for leadership of the working class. Organized but a few years previously and built on the basis of all that was militant and revolutionary in the traditions and experiences of the American and international labor movement, the Trade Union Unity League began to emerge as the new leader of the American workers, the only trade union leadership which presented a consistent program of struggle in the sharpening situation.

The crisis, resting its deadly burden upon the workers, called forth actions which were unprecedented even in the fierce class struggle of previous years. With an increase in the militancy of the workers—egged on by severe wagecuts and unemployment—the repressive measures of the ruling class were sharpened. Textile strikers in Lawrence and

Paterson were attacked mercilessly by police and thugs. In Chicago three and in Cleveland two unemployed Negro workers were murdered by police at demonstrations against evictions. Four Detroit workers were shot down and killed in front of the Ford plant in Dearborn by the private police army of Henry Ford and the police of the liberal Mayor Murphy of Detroit when a large crowd of unemployed workers marched on the plant to demand the jobs the "wonder of America" had promised them but a week before. In the bituminous coal fields of western Pennsylvania, eastern Ohio and West Virginia, 40,000 miners took up the struggle under the leadership of the National Miners' Union, which had first entered the field in 1928 as the direct inheritor of all that was really militant in the traditions of the miners.

The fiercest battle yet fought was in the coal fields of southeastern Kentucky, where the National Miners' Union led the workers in a bitter struggle against the same semifeudal conditions which roused the resistance of the Molly Maguires in the Pennsylvania anthracite over a half century ago. Some of the biggest coal interests in the country dominated the coal fields with an army of hundreds of armed thugs. Strikers were shot down, their homes raided; they were thrust into prison, framed on murder, charged and tried for criminal syndicalism. As in previous struggles the leadership of the United Mine Workers of America—now open strike-breakers—took sides with the operators against the miners.

From the time of the Mollies the list of martyrs in the class struggle has grown into the hundreds. It is the dynamics of the class struggle that makes out of these victims of capitalism martyrs of the working class. Hangings, shootings, oppression have not spelled defeat for the workers. They have only increased working class resistance, strengthened its sinews for renewed and more highly developed struggles.

Over the stretch of years which separates us from the Mollies, the American working class has gained much in tradition and experience. With the growth of a conscious revolutionary movement led by the Communist Party sectional isolation becomes less and less possible. Struggles, no matter in what part of the country, no matter of what section of the working class, no longer remain isolated or purely sectional as was the case with the Molly Maguires. They are taken up as a part of the struggle of the whole working class, which comes to the support of the workers with relief, defense and other actions of solidarity.

No longer an isolated national section under imperialism, the American working class also partakes of the experiences of other countries. More and more, internationalism becomes a prerequisite for the successful waging of working class struggles in any country. The experiences of the proletarian revolution and the successful building of Socialism in the Soviet Union no longer leaves the question of the struggle for the abolition of the capitalist system a mute problem. Every strike, every labor struggle, carries the seeds of this problem buried in its soil. With every struggle in this epoch these seeds become more firmly embedded and take root. They are watered by the ever more glaring contradictions revealed to the workers in the use of the state power by the employers in their attempts to crush every struggle. These seeds are nurtured by experience, from the Molly Maguires to Kentucky and Scottsboro and the Soviet Union.

When the operators of the anthracite region of Pennsylvania murdered the Molly Maguires they were but helping to create the conditions for the overthrow of the system of capitalist exploitation and oppression.

REFERENCE NOTES

1. *History of Schuylkill County, Pa.*, Anonymous, published by W. W. Munsell & Co., New York, 1881, p. 99.
2. *Irish World*, New York, June 30, 1877.
3. J. F. Patterson, "The Old W.B.A." and "After the W.B.A." in *Historical Society of Schuylkill County, Pa. Publications,* Vols. II and IV.
4. Chris Evans, *History of the United Mine Workers of America,* Vol. 2, 1918.
5. James Oneal, *The Workers in American History,* Fourth Edit., p. 181.
6. *Speeches of Eugene V. Debs,* Voices of Revolt, Vol. IX, p. 76.
7. Peter Roberts, *Anthracite Coal Communities,* 1904, p. 12.
8. F. P. Dewees, *The Molly Maguires,* 1877, p. 16.
9. *Ibid.,* pp. 20-21.
10. *Ibid.,* p. 17.
11. Quoted by Alexander Trachtenberg in his *History of the Legislation for the Protection of Coal Miners in Pennsylvania* (unpublished manuscript of doctoral dissertation, Yale University Library, 1914).
12. *Reports of the Inspectors of Coal Miners of the Anthracite Regions of Pennsylvania for the year 1871,* pp. 114-124.
13. *Ibid.,* 1875, p. 8.
14. Peter Roberts, *The Anthracite Coal Industry,* 1901, p. 109.
15. Trachtenberg, *op. cit.*
16. *Ibid.*
17. Roberts, *The Anthracite Coal Industry,* p. 148.
18. *Ibid.,* p. 100.
19. Most of the songs are taken from George G. Korson's, *Song's and Ballads of the Anthracite Miner,* 1927, pp. 75-83.
20. Roberts, *The Anthracite Coal Industry,* p. 19.
21. Charles A. Beard and Mary R. Beard, *The Rise of American Civilization,* 1927, Vol. II, p. 108.
22. *Ibid.,* p. 106.
23. *Ibid.,* p. 71.
24. Commons and Associates, *History of Labor in the United States,* Vol. II, 1921, p. 109.
25. Anna Rochester, *Labor and Coal,* 1931, p. 165.
26. *History of Schuylkill County,* published by W. W. Munsell & Co., New York, 1881, p. 97.
27. Trachtenberg, *op. cit.*
28. Peter Roberts, *The Anthracite Coal Industry,* 1901, pp. 172-173.
29. Chris Evans, *op. cit.,* Vol. I, p. 7.
30. *Ibid.,* Vol. I, pp. 14-15.

31. Andrew Roy, *History of the Coal Miners of the United States,*
    1907, p. 78.
32. Dewees, *op. cit.*, pp. 30-31.
33. Quoted by Ashtown, *The Unknown Power Behind the Irish Na-*
    tionalist Party, 1908, p. 34.
34. James Connolly, *Labor in Irish History*, 1910, p. 26.
35. *Collections in Irish Church History,* From the Manuscript of the
    Late Rev. Lawrence F. Renehan, D.D., 1874, pp. 335-336.
36. James Connolly, *op. cit.*, p. 57.
37. Richard Robert Madden, *The United Irishmen*, 1916, pp. 262-263.
38. Dewees, *op. cit.*, pp. 24-25.
39. *Ibid.*, p. 34.
40. A. K. McClure, *Old Time Notes of Pennsylvania*, 1905, p. 433.
41. Dewees, *op. cit.*, p. 32.
42. *Arguments of Franklin B. Gowen, Esq., of Counsel for the Com-*
    monwealth, in the case of the Commonwealth vs. Thomas Munley,
    p. 21.
43. Dewees, *op. cit.*, p. 34.
44. *Ibid.*, p. 230.
45. *Miners' National Record*, May, 1875.
46. See Anna Rochester's *Labor and Coal* for a full description of the
    policies of the officialdom of the United Mine Workers of America.
47. *Miners' National Record*, October, 1875.
48. *Ibid.*, July, 1875.
49. *Ibid.*, July, 1875.
50. *Ibid.*, June, 1875.
51. Reprinted by the *Miners' National Record*, June, 1875.
52. Dewees, *op. cit.*, pp. 121-122.
53. J. F. Patterson, "The Old W. B. A.," in *Historical Society of*
    Schuylkill County, Pa. Publications, Vol. II, p. 366.
54. Evans, *op. cit.*, Vol. I, p. 81.
55. Patterson, "After the W. B. A.," *op. cit.*, Vol. IV, pp. 168-184.
56. *Report of the Case of the Commonwealth vs. John Kehoe and*
    others, pp. 176-180.
57. Dewees, *op. cit.*, p. 73.
58. Roberts, *The Anthracite Coal Industry*, 1901, p. 251.
59. Allan Pinkerton, *The Molly Maguires and the Detectives*, 1878,
    pp. 259-260.
60. Evans, *op. cit.*, Vol. I, p. 61.
61. *MacMillan's Magazine*, December, 1896.
62. Andrew Roy, *op. cit.*
63. Trachtenberg, *op. cit.*
64. *Ibid.*
65. Dewees, *op. cit.*, pp. 348-350.
66. *Arguments of F. B. Gowen, Esq.*, p. 22.
67. *Ibid.*, p. 16.
68. See *Spying on Workers*, by Robert W. Dunn (International
    Pamphlets, 1932), for full description of the labor spy system.
69. *Miner's Weekly Journal*, July 21, 1876.
70. *Arguments of F. B. Gowen, Esq.*, p. 31.

71. For a detailed account of the conspiracy against the Western Federation of Miners see *Bill Haywood's Book*, 1929, Chaps. XI and XII.
72. *The Commonwealth vs. John Kehoe*, p. 193.
73. T. F. McGrath, *History of the Ancient Order of Hibernians*, 1898, p. 60.
74. *Daily Miners' Journal*, July 3, 1876.
75. Dewees, *op. cit.*, p. 230.
76. *Daily Miners' Journal*, January 31, 1876.
77. *Ibid.*, January 31, 1876.
78. *Ibid.*, February 2, 1876.
79. *Ibid.*, July 2, 1876.
80. *Ibid.*, February 8, 1876.
81. *Lives and Crimes of the Molly Maguires*, Anom., p. 35.
82. *Daily Miners' Journal*, May 6, 1876.
83. *The Great Molly Maguire Trials in Carbon and Schuylkill Counties, Pa.*, Chronicle Book and Job Rooms, Pottsville, Pa., p. 29.
84. *Miners' Daily Journal*, May 8, 1876.
85. *Ibid.*, May 11, 1876.
86. *Ibid.*, May, 1876.
87. *The Great Molly Maguire Trials*, p. 18.
88. *Ibid.*, p. 20.
89. *Daily Miners' Journal*, May, 1876.
90. *Ibid.*, pp. 9-10.
91. *Lives and Crimes of the Molly Maguires*, p. 51.
92. *Arguments of Franklin B. Gowen, Esq.*, p. 19.
93. *Ibid.*, pp. 9-10.
94. *Ibid.*, p. 5.
95. *Ibid.*, p. 6.
96. *Ibid.*, p. 4.
97. *Ibid.*, p. 6.
98. *Ibid.*, pp. 7-8.
99. *Daily Miners' Journal*, July 11, 1876.
100. *Ibid.*, July, 1876.
101. *Daily Miners' Journal*, July 13, 1876.
102. *Arguments of F. B. Gowen, Esq.*, pp. 24, 33-34, 35-36.
103. *Daily Miners' Journal*, July 13, 1876.
104. *Ibid.*
105. Dewees, *op. cit.*
106. *The Commonwealth vs. Kehoe*, pp. 129, 134.
107. *Lives and Crimes of the Molly Maguires*, p. 100.
108. *Patrick Hester, et al. vs. Commonwealth of Pennsylvania*, Bloomsburg, Pa. Library, p. 23.
109. *Ibid.*, pp. 24-25.
110. *Ibid.*, p. 518.
111. *Ibid.*
112. *Frank Leslie's Illustrated Newspaper*, July 7, 1877.
113. *Lives and Crimes of the Molly Maguires*, p. 43.
114. Dewees, *op. cit.*, p. 35.
115. Rollins Edwards, *Twice Defeated*, pp. 421-423.
116. *Labor Standard*, February 24, 1877.
117. New York *Sun*, January 14, 1877.

INDEX

A

Albright, General, 87, 88, 89, 92, 98.

American Federation of Labor, 57, 130.

American Legion, 132.

American Miners' Association, 41-42.

Ancient Order of Hibernians, and anthracite miners, 11-12, 47, 54; as organizational center of miners, 54, 67, 124; attitude of operators to, 51, 52-53; constitution of, 46; in politics, 52; Irish background of, 46, 47-51.

Andrews, Richard, 107.

Anthracite miners, conditions of, 18 ff; songs about, 29-30; strikes of, 26, 27, 36-37, 39, 43, 54 ff, 131.

Anthracite Region of Pennsylvania, British capital in, 61, 75; migrations to and population in, 18-19; production of coal in, 19; starvation in, 68, 73; settlements in, 20.

Appeal to Reason, 17.

B

Barkoski, John, 133.

Bates, John, 39, 40.

Bates Union, 39, 40.

Beatty, Sergeant, 50.

Bituminous miners, strike of, 58.

Blacklist, 65, 87; songs about, 65-66.

Boylan, John, 130.

Boyle, James, 92, 94, 116, 119.

British miners, conditions of, 74-75.

Brown, D. J., 79.

C

Campbell, Alexander, 85-86, 91, 98, 116, 120.

Carroll, James, 91, 98, 116, 120.

Catholic Church, and anthracite miners, 75-76, 77, 123; in Ireland, 49; and Pinkertons, 75, 77.

Centralia Case, 83, 125, 132.

Chartist Movement, 40.

Child labor in mines, description of, 30-32; percentage of, 32; songs about, 32.

Civil War, and development of capitalism, 34 ff, 122; and price of coal, 28; and wages, 28.

Coal and Iron Police, 55, 83, 89.

Coal Companies, financiers and, 33; Lehigh and Wilkes-Barre, 87, 92, 97; Long Strike and, 57; Railroads and, 33; Philadelphia and Reading Railroad and, 33-34, 55; songs about, 65; trials and, 87, 88-89, 98-99.

Coyle, Edward, 71.

Cromwellian Conquest, 47-48.

Cull, Manus, 112-114.

Cummings, Mathew, 47.

D

Debs, Eugene V., 17, 132.

Defense of miners in court, 88-89, 108, 126-127, 128, 129.

Donahue, John, 116, 120.

Donahue, Thomas, 111.

Dougherty, Daniel, 84.

Doyle, Michael, 102.

Doyle, Michael J., 85, 86, 88, 90, 102, 116, 120.

Duffy, John, 111.

Duffy, Thomas, 92, 100, 116, 120.